Michele~

Thank You for all you do! Happy Holidays.

Kim & Brittany

THE SHEPHERD'S CROSS

A Christmas Carol of Hope

THE SHEPHERD'S CROSS

A Christmas Carol of Hope

BY GARY E. PARKER

Run So That You May Win
ivictor.com

Victor is an imprint of
Cook Communications Ministries, Colorado Springs, Colorado
80918
Cook Communications, Paris, Ontario
Kingsway Communications, Eastbourne, England

THE SHEPHERD'S CROSS
© 2001 by Gary Parker

First Printing, 2001
Printed in the United States of America

1 2 3 4 5 6 7 8 9 10 Printing/Year 05 04 03 02 01

Sr. Editor: Craig Bubeck
Cover Design: Matthew C. DeCoste
Interior Design: Matthew C. DeCoste

Unless otherwise noted, Scripture quotations are
taken from the Holy Bible: New International Version®.
Copyright © 1973, 1978, 1984 by International Bible Society.
Used by permission of Zondervan Publishing House.
All rights reserved.

Library of Congress Cataloging-in-Publication Data

Parker, Gary
Shepherd's Cross/Gary Parker

p. cm.
ISBN 078143694X

Contents

1

SAD THINGS

The clouds had congregated all day, their brooding gray faces hanging low over the ground. A whippy wind tugged at their edges, its gusts twirling the shriveled remnants of the year's leaves up and down in the air. They made a skittering sound on the street as they passed, like a skeleton's bones being dragged over a bed of small rocks. The residents of Buckview, a two-red-light mountain town in western North Carolina, kept looking up as they hustled to and fro on the one main street, their eyes busy surveying the weather, their necks jammed as far as possible into their heavy coats, scarves, and jackets. Everyone commented that snow would no doubt commence before the dark fell, but somehow that notion didn't make folks smile as it usually did. For some reason, the approaching snow seemed threatening, almost as if it had a score to settle with somebody and would do so before Christmas morning.

At just past five-twenty on Saturday afternoon a bell tinkled over the door of Turley's Hardware. Chipper

Gaines, a young man about the size of a typical high school second baseman, stepped out of the store and onto the sidewalk. Wearing a pair of worn but clean jeans, a waist-length brown jacket turned up at the collar, and a navy baseball cap, Chipper held a red bicycle to his chest. A dog the color of a moonless night trailed after him, his head almost to Chipper's waist, his tongue a thick pink string puffing white breath into the air.

Surprised by the frigid wind, Chipper suddenly stopped and stared up at the clouds. The dog braked too. A single string of Christmas lights—bulbs alternating red, then green, red, green—suddenly blinked on over the street. The lights seemed to quiver in the wind for a moment. Then one of them popped, and sparks flew out from it—all the lights blinked, blinked, blinked, and flickered off. Pushed by the wind, a thin piece of broken tree branch brushed against the back of Chipper's legs as the lights went out, and he spun around at the unseen attacker, the bicycle almost falling from his grasp. Seeing the branch, he smiled sheepishly.

"Spooky out here, Thumper," he said to the dog, his pale gray eyes back on the sky. "Let's go see Ty Bo, then take it to the house." The dog wagged his tail in agreement, and Chipper headed across the street toward a beat-up brown truck, its pedigree so ruined by age and wear that the chrome name plate over the front grill had fallen off. A spot of rust the size of a football chewed away on the right back fender, and the tires were as thin as potato skins. But like everything else about Chipper Gaines, the truck was well-washed, even in the dead of winter.

His right hand cold on the handlebars, Chipper hefted the bicycle toward the truck bed. At the same time, he balanced the body of the bike on his left arm—his left stump actually, a stump with almost nothing past the elbow. Using it as a stabilizer, he eased the bike into the back of the truck. Hurrying, he dropped a piece of faded canvas over the bike, placed a thick rock on each corner, clicked at Thumper, and jumped after him into the cab. Pulling his cap lower, Chipper zipped up his jacket, blew on his right hand, and hit the ignition. A bad spring jabbed at his back through what remained of the truck's plastic seat covers and the heater refused to work, but Chipper paid neither of the inconveniences any attention.

Steering with his knees and stump, he shifted gears with his right hand, pulled away from the hardware store and pointed the truck south toward Asheville, almost eleven miles away. Thumper sat tall on the passenger seat, like a ship's navigator.

Shivering, Chipper glanced in the rear view mirror at the bike. He noticed his reflection. He had simple but strong features—a square chin, an unremarkable nose, and eyebrows as blonde as his hair. People who knew him said the most remarkable thing about his appearance was his eyes, how they seemed older than his twenty-seven years, sadder at the edges than they deserved. But tonight the eyes weren't sad. Tonight was Christmas Eve, and he'd just bought his son the best gift a boy could ever receive.

Blinking, Chipper stared back at the road. The clouds now reached down to the gravel and covered it like a blanket settling in for a long night. A gust of wind suddenly grabbed the steering wheel and jerked the truck toward the road's edge—Chipper fought to pull it back. Thumper whined. The sense of foreboding he'd felt on the street returned. The night seemed poised, its body curled like a snake about to strike. Chipper shuddered.

"Home in a jiffy," he said to Thumper, his tone cheerier than he felt. "Home for Christmas." Chipper turned right and headed up a steep incline. His stump ached in the cold, and in spite of his efforts to the contrary, his mood continued to darken. Bad weather meant bad times for him and his family.

He and his wife Reba and their two children—Kyle Lee, nearly nine; and Andrea Grace, two—lived in a rented, four-room wood house about halfway up a dirt road in what everybody in Buckview called a "holler." A single, cast iron stove—fit for coal or wood—heated the whole house. The caulking on the windows had long since lost its hold and the hardwood floors had no insulation under them. Only one room, the center one that people saw as they entered, had anything resembling a rug, and that thing—a round piece the color of pine bark—looked more suited for a dog than a human. And though Chipper kept a good stack of wood by the back door, he knew that if ice or snow really hit and the roads closed down for more than three or four days, he'd run low in a hurry.

The truck rounded a sharp curve and a clutter of black birds flew past the hood, their wings a whir beating against the almost-black sky. Apparently chasing the birds, a gray cat the size of a raccoon pounced across the road, its green eyes catching Chipper's for an instant as it glanced his way. The cat's eyes seemed to see right through him, and he had the crazy feeling that the animal was reading his mind. With a high-pitched screech the cat disappeared into a patch of high brush on the far side of the road.

Chipper's chin dropped lower. Times were hard for men like him—men with a streak of red, white, and blue running through their spines, a streak that had compelled them to drop out of school and enlist in the army when the big war came.

Chipper jammed his stump against his side and fussed at himself for feeling gloomy. No reason to fret, especially not tonight. He checked the rear view mirror again, and his spirits momentarily lifted. He had some blessings he could count. A loving family waited for him at home—even as poor a house as it was. And, unless he missed his guess, Reba had something hot cooked up for supper, maybe corn bread and pinto beans and potato salad made with onions, just like he liked it. Maybe best of all, he had just made the last of eight, two-dollar-fifty-cents-a-month lay-away payments on a red bicycle for Kyle Lee—a bike with a horn, a tassel on each hand grip; and white-wall tires. The boy had wanted the bike for over two years, and Chipper had worked a second job every Saturday as a checking clerk at Turley's for the last four months to pay for it. He was prouder of his purchasing that bike than maybe anything he'd ever done, except marry Reba and father his kids.

Chipper smiled. Reba had married him right before the war, May 1, 1942, to be exact—a "marry-me-before-I-go-off-to-get-shot" bride like thousands of others who said their vows one week and shipped their husbands off the next. Though only eighteen at the time, Chip and Reba had known each other all their days, their lives as intertwined as the roots under one of the maple trees that flourished on the mountain slopes. He knew her better than the back of his hand—the way she combed her wavy black hair to show off the bluest eyes in the county; the way she clogged, her toes bouncing off the floor quick as a flea jumping; the sweetness of her soprano voice rising from the choir at the Baptist church where she sang every Sunday.

Chipper steered the truck down a steep slope. Thoughts of Reba faded, and his spirits sagged again. The cold sank deeper into his body. He wished the heater worked. He checked the bike again in hopes of recapturing his upbeat mood. But, thinking of the church where Reba sang, his emotions refused to cooperate—the sadness that he hated, but knew far too well, was once more wrapping its bony fingers around his throat.

Just as he knew Reba, she knew him, too—knew that he didn't go to church much anymore. Hadn't felt fit since he returned from the war. Hadn't felt quite right sitting on the hard-backed pews, listening to the sermons, shaking hands with all the good people who attended there. A man who goes to war comes back different, no doubt about it, and that difference wasn't always for the good.

Chipper glanced at his stump. Not only had the war kept him from a proper education, but it had also claimed a significant part of himself. The missing piece of the arm still ached at times—a throb in the emptiness between the elbow that remained and the forearm, wrist, hand, and fingertips that didn't. He used to joke grimly about his "aching void," but neither he nor anybody else really saw any humor in it.

Seeing a peeling white fence, Chipper turned right, and parked under a trio of bare oak trees. For several long seconds, he stayed still, his head spinning. His missing arm wasn't the only ache he'd felt since the war. For that matter, it wasn't the only thing he'd left behind. Though he didn't recognize it at the time, he seemed to have lost his innocence there too—slivers and slices of it scattered on the ground of the green-leafed jungle where he had done most of his fighting.

Shaking his head, Chipper suddenly felt a shuddering need for a drink. He licked his lips. Just a small drink, he figured—one swig to pick him up, help him fight through the holidays. Heck, he hadn't taken a drink in over twelve months—not since . . . He brushed off the memory, his mouth watering. No harm in just one shot, a voice in his head said. But then he bit his lip until it almost bled and steeled himself against the temptation. He WOULD NOT DO THAT AGAIN! He could not do that again! Not after last time, not after all the promises he'd made. Nausea rolled through his stomach, and he forced his mind away from the taste of alcohol.

He heard a tip tap, tip tap, tip tap on top of the truck and realized it had started sleeting. Blowing on his fingers, he patted Thumper on the head.

"Back in a minute," he said. Thumper whined in protest but then lay down. Chipper hopped out and hustled across the muddy drive and up three steps onto a wood stoop on the side of a large but simple gray house. The structure served as both the office and home of Mr. Ty Bo Shiller, a sixty-year-old logger with a hefty wife and three grown children. Ty Bo owned four trucks, eight chain saws, more axes than anyone had ever bothered to count, and enough logging chain, cords, and ropes to hang every cow in the county if he had a mind to do such a thing.

Chipper worked for Shiller but not as a logger. Unable to do heavy labor because of his missing arm, Chipper performed a variety of other chores. He kept what little paper work Ty Bo bothered to file, hauled sandwiches and cold drinks to the other four men he employed, and assisted the mechanic who kept all of Ty Bo's machinery running. Every now and again, when someone turned up sick, Chipper actually jumped behind the wheel of one of the monster logging trucks, his stump working in tandem with his knees to keep the rig on the road while he shifted gears with his right hand. He didn't do that often and he drove slowly when he did, but what a challenge!

Popping back the door, he saw Ty Bo sitting behind a small square desk, a single lamp hanging from the wall, and a stack of papers.

"Close the dad-gum door!" shouted Ty Bo, not looking up. "Freeze me to death!"

Chipper slammed the door.

"You done with everything?" asked Ty Bo, his eyes on a pad, a pair of glasses perched on his wide nose.

Chipper moved to the coal stove in the center of the room and held his hand over it. "Yeah, picked up the whole list," he said, feeling good about his work. "Oil for the trucks, a new tire, belts for the chainsaws . . ." he recited the items Ty Bo had sent him to retrieve. "When we get back after Christmas, we're primed and ready to work."

Ty Bo raised his eyes over his glasses, rolled his ample shoulders. "Sit down, son," he said, pointing to a hard chair by the desk. "How long you been working for me?"

Though not sure why, Chipper suddenly felt nervous. His stump started to hurt as he took a seat. He stuck his hand in his pocket.

"Four years," he said. "Come on here the second year after the war ended."

"I've done right by you, haven't I?" asked Ty Bo.

"Sure, Mr. Shiller. We work good together, I've learned a lot."

Shiller sighed, lay his glasses on the desk, slapped his hands on his knees and stood. His body towered over the desk, his girth the width of a horse's rump. He edged around the desk, parked on the corner.

"I got a son," he said, staring at the floor.

"I know," said Chipper. "Off to college over at State."

Ty Bo rubbed his hairless head. "He's comin' home this week," he said. "Finished all his courses at college. Lookin' to come into business with me, wants to take this loggin' work and make it a real enterprise."

Chipper pulled off his hat, hung it on a knee. "Be good to see Rodney again," he said. "How long since he come home?"

"'Bout a year. He worked with the State Forestry Agency last summer." Ty Bo wiped his chin, studied the floor as if looking for gold in the cracks of the hardwood planks. Chipper heard the coal in the stove shift.

"I can't keep you on," said Ty Bo. "Not with Rodney comin' home. Can't afford the two of you." He talked quickly, as if rushing the words would make them easier to swallow. "He's got to learn the business from the bottom up, do the stuff you been doin'. I been tryin' to figure out how to make it work, but it's slow times— you know that. Loggin' is tough right now; it's all I can do to keep body and soul together." He stopped and moved to the stove, his back to it. Chipper felt numb, his tongue stilled by shock. Ty Bo continued his speech.

"I know it's bad tellin' you this right 'fore Christmas, but I didn't want to wait until the New Year and have you comin' in here like everything was okay. Figured you could start lookin' now, maybe find something in a week or so, be ready to go after the holiday."

Ty Bo took a breath, and Chipper picked his hat off his knee, dangled it on his fingers. Inside his head, a thousand thoughts swirled, but he couldn't make any order out of any of them. They just bunched up all together, one bad feeling after the next, a swarm of hurts and aches like a cloud of locusts, each of them eating at him from his guts on out.

He'd failed Reba, he realized, failed her again. Not only did he have a compulsion for the drink, but he couldn't take care of his family either—not like he wanted, not like they deserved. A wave of guilt crashed over him. He was no good—lower than dirt under a porch, a no-account excuse of a man who couldn't even hold the one job his lowly qualifications had allowed him to perform. He stared at the floor, his shoulders slumped in shame. The desire for a drink climbed to the back of his throat and hung there like a man clinging to a ledge for dear life. The urge for liquor made Chipper shiver and he shoved his hat back on and looked up at Ty Bo, his eyes fierce, not so much at Schiller but at himself, at his inability to provide for his family.

"You tellin' me I got no job?" he asked, unable to believe what he'd heard.

Ty Bo moved to him, placed a thick hand on his back. His eyes were moist. "You're a good worker," he said. "Most dependable man I got. I tell you to do somethin', you do it, eager as a beaver. You smart, too; quick as a whip on the learnin'. But my work needs . . . well . . . you know . . . I need stout men . . . men who—"

Chipper threw up his hand to stop him. He knew the type of men Ty Bo needed—whole men, men with two full arms. He dropped his hand to a knee.

"Maybe I can use you again in the spring," said Ty Bo. "Loggin' always picks up in the spring."

For several seconds, the two men stayed as they were, as stiff as the stumps they left behind after they sawed down a tree. The coal in the stove shifted again. The room seemed to grow colder—as cold as an icehouse now—so cold it seemed to freeze up every good feeling Chipper had ever felt. His heart felt like an ice cycle.

He took a breath, then lay his hand over Ty Bo's hand, as if to comfort him. The only sound in the room was the click, click, click of sleet on the roof. Chipper patted Ty Bo's hand, then pushed it off his shoulder and stood.

"I need to get on," he said. "Reba be waitin'."

Ty Bo nodded, picked an envelope off his desk. "Take this," he said. "Your check. Plus a . . . well, a touch more, tide you over maybe."

Not looking in the envelope, Chipper pushed it into his jacket pocket and headed to the door. Opening it, he faced Ty Bo once more.

"I'm thankin' you for the work," he said. "You been a friend."

"I'm still a friend," said Ty Bo. "You okay?"

Chipper studied his boots, his gut craving a shot of something hot and bitter. He remembered the last drink he'd taken, just over twelve months ago—December 10, the day of his daddy's funeral. That one had been twenty years to the month since his mama's burial. He had fought the urge to drink all through his daddy's service, but then—his soul aching—he gave in and took up a neighbor's offer for a beer. One beer, he thought. A man needs a drink when his daddy dies. But that one beer was all it took for another sickening spiral into hell to begin.

The first beer just plain tasted good. So good, in fact, he decided to try another—just one more. At that point, a twinge of guilt hit him. But he quickly pushed it aside. A man didn't need to feel guilty over two beers. He held at two beers for about thirty minutes, but then Reba smelled the drink on his breath and griped to him about it. That gave him the excuse he needed to go for a third. A wife ought to understand, he reasoned, ought to understand when a man is grieving and leave him be. He sucked down a third beer and then a shot of whiskey. The guilt worsened. But it was too late to stop now. If you're going to feel guilty, he decided, you might as well give yourself a good reason for it. He took another glass of whiskey to wash out the guilt. But it didn't help.

Before he knew what had happened, the guilt did what it always seemed to do when he drank. It shifted itself into anger—anger at all the opportunities he'd never had, the bad luck that always seemed to find him no matter how hard he tried to avoid it. His past boiled up like hot lava, and he lost himself in a fog of hurt that grabbed him by the hand and pulled him into the black hole of an alcoholic binge for four days, his whole body consumed by whiskey. His—

"Chipper?"

Ty Bo's kindly voice broke through his thoughts.

"Yeah, . . . I'm . . . I'm okay," he stammered, though not feeling okay at all.

"Come see me in the spring,"

"I better be working somewhere else in the spring," said Chipper. "Doctor said Reba's due for delivery of our new baby in April."

"I'll pray for you."

"I don't need prayers," said Chipper. "What I need is a job."

Turning, he slammed the door and stepped off the stoop. His shoulders hunched against the sleet, he climbed into his truck, ignored Thumper, and hit the ignition. The engine sputtered, then caught, but Chipper didn't pull out right away. As the sleet clattered down he licked his lips, his whole body desperate for a shot of something to numb his mind. Shoving his stump into his side, he fought against the urge, his mind at war with his cravings.

Before the war he'd never tasted strong drink, not

even once. Though he had some uncles famous for a homemade elixir that some said could make a sick man well or melt paint—whichever you needed—he'd stayed away from the stuff his whole life. But then the war came—almost four years of . . . well, a body didn't talk about all that. Suffice it to say, though, his time in the jungles of the Pacific had provided him more than enough cause to acquire a taste for just about anything with a bite or a burn.

Thumper pushed his nose against his leg. Chipper patted the dog on the head.

"You ready to go home?"

Thumper's tail banged on the seat.

"You right, boy. We'll go home real soon." He pulled out of the drive, his mind busy trying to figure how to tell Reba he'd lost his job. No good way came to him. He moved onto the highway, his spirits falling with each spin of the tires. Ever since he'd returned from the war, he and his family had lived on the edges of poverty. But he'd always managed to keep a job, often two for that matter, and the jobs had paid him enough to not only keep the wolf away from the door but to gradually draw ahead a little. But now this—a bad time for the mountain economy and him laid off. The urge for a drink again rolled up, and this time it hit him so hard he knew it was useless to fight it anymore. One drink couldn't hurt anything.

"Just one," he said to Thumper, his mind decided. "One to get me over this bad spot.
I got hard work to do tonight, hard work."

Thumper whined, but Chipper ignored the disapproval. The sleet pounded down even harder now, and the road was quickly glazing over. For a moment, he remembered the truck's bad tires but then shrugged it off. When a man has a thousand problems to worry about, one more doesn't make much difference. The truck easing through the sleety night, and Chipper Gaines, a good man with a tragic weakness, gave over to his urges and licked his lips in anticipation of a good stiff drink.

2

BAD CHOICES

*H*is chewing gum busy, Chipper quietly followed Thumper through the front door of his home and hung his hat on a nail. The smell of fresh bread filled his nostrils, overwhelming the aroma of wood smoke that usually dominated the room. To his right sat the Christmas tree, a cedar he and Kyle Lee had chopped down six days ago. The tree's boughs were decorated with popcorn strings and red bows that Reba had fashioned from a worn-out dress. Underneath the tree lay a stack of presents—not large, but enough to make him feel good about working so hard. A new Bible for Reba—she swore her old one was worn out, plus a blue blouse to match her eyes. A baseball, a couple of shirts, and a new pair of jeans for Kyle Lee. A baby doll, a dress, and bonnet for Andrea Grace.

A wood stove sat across from the tree, its black belly pushing out heat like a boiler producing steam. Though sleet clattered on the windows and wind riffled around the corners of the house, the room felt unnaturally warm to Chipper and his face was flushed.

Patting the left pocket of his jacket, he felt the bottle there and knew the source of the heat. Booze always warmed him up, made his usually pale skin come alive with color. He'd had about a third of the bottle so far, not enough to make him drunk, but enough to relax his tensions a little, enough to make him feel bolder. He'd need that to tell Reba about Ty Bo, about—

"I'm in the kitchen," shouted Reba from behind a door straight ahead. "The coffee is hot."

Chipper slipped a new piece of gum into his mouth as the kitchen door popped open and Kyle Lee ran toward him, his blonde hair a mop in his eyes, his hands stretched out like he was about to catch a baseball. Chipper dropped to his knees, grabbed the boy, and the lifted him up in the air, the two of them spinning around and around.

"Mama's makin' apple pie!" shouted Kyle Lee. "Apples come from Mrs. Branch—down at the church. A whole basket of red apples. Most got no worms at all!"

Laughing, Chipper eased Kyle Lee to the floor, took his hand and headed to the kitchen, Thumper trailing. Reba stopped working as they entered. Her hands were white with flour, a smidge of it on her right cheek, and even more on her apron. It rounded out a touch in the middle, a visible sign of her third pregnancy. Chipper started to kiss her but then remembered his breath and ducked away toward the sink.

"I'm starvin'," he said, his eyes on the floor.

"Supper will be ready in about thirty minutes," said Reba. "Got a nice hen from Maxy's." Reba waved at the small electric stove at her back. "Take a biscuit. It'll tide you over."

Careful not to step too close, he pulled three biscuits off a plate, poured a cup of coffee, and took a swig. "You want some?" he asked, looking for the sugar bowl.

"Nope—I've had my cup for the day."

"Andrea Grace nappin'?" He faced the table, leaned against the stove.

"Snug as a bug in a rug. I'll wake her when supper's ready."

For several seconds Chipper watched Reba work. A petite woman, she had a figure as prim as a baby doll. Her eyes were as blue as the water in Ruffin Lake in August, and she had skin so white it looked like skim milk.

Chipper sighed. Though he didn't believe in miracles, the fact that Reba had actually married him came as close to one as anything he knew. She had so many things he didn't have—a high school diploma plus a couple of years of community college, two living parents who made good, a touch of sophistication without stuffiness, fine grammar in her speech . . .

"Kyle Lee wants to go to bed early," said Reba, interrupting his thoughts.

Chipper nodded at his son. "Santa can't come until all the kids are all asleep," he said, tossing the boy a biscuit and laying one on the floor for Thumper. "No sleep, no Santa." He joined Kyle Lee at the table, his chair turned backwards, his legs astride it.

"Santa gone bring me my bike this year?" asked Kyle Lee, eyes aglow.

"Depends on you, I guess," said Chipper, his smile wide, his mood lightened by the whiskey in his stomach.

"You been a good boy?"

Kyle Lee nodded. "Most times."

"What you say to that, Mrs. Gaines?" Chipper asked, turning to Reba. "He tellin' it true?"

Reba smiled, and the room seemed to brighten by several watts. She stepped to her son and touched his forehead, leaving a white splotch the shape of a finger print between his eyes. "Most times is right," she beamed. "Good enough for a shiny new bike, it seems to me. Now eat your biscuit." She focused on her work again.

Chipper grinned happily, his spirits rising in spite of the troubles he hadn't yet explained to Reba. Without thinking, he took out his gum. Not sure where to put it, he rolled it in his fingers for a moment. Reba saw it. Her hands fell still in the flour bowl. A shadow seemed to wrap around the room. Realizing his mistake, Chipper grabbed his coffee cup, but felt it grow cold in his hand. Reba knew he only chewed gum when—

Her voice sounded unusually calm when she spoke, but her hands still didn't move. "Go check on your sister," she said to Kyle Lee. "Stay with her until I come for you."

Obviously knowing the tone, the boy obeyed without argument, Thumper at his heels. Chipper broke off a piece of biscuit and put it in his mouth, but didn't chew. Reba wiped her hands on her apron and joined him at the table. Chipper examined the rest of the biscuit as if expecting to see it turn into a diamond. Reba took the biscuit, laid it on a plate. Then she put her hand on his.

"Did you stop on the way home from Ty Bo's?" she asked, her voice gentle but firm.

"Yeah," he said, eyes still on the biscuit. "But only for a minute."

She nodded, obviously knowing what that meant. "Look," she said. "I hate to have to ask you this, but . . ." she sighed heavily, "Did you bring home your check?"

Chipper's head dropped lower. The last time had been a Saturday, too, and he'd spent every dime in his pockets. Reba had been forced to go to her parents and borrow money, something both of them hated. The Fullers were nice folks, but it seemed to Chipper that they'd always kept a certain distance from him, Mr. Fuller especially. Middle class folks—Mr. Fuller worked at an Asheville bank, Mrs. Fuller as a secretary at a doctor's office—they seemed uncomfortable with the fact that their only daughter had taken up with a low-class boy whose daddy worked at a gas station and lived on a side of town that no one really called respectable.

A hint of indignation flared up in Chipper. What right did the Fullers have to look down their noses at him?

"Check's in my jacket," he said, a touch resentful of the question. "Safe and sound."

Reba nodded and patted his hand, a thin smile on her lips. Chipper chewed on the biscuit in his mouth but hardly tasted it.

"You promised me," said Reba.

"I know," he said, eager to explain. "But I got things on my mind, things—

"Nothing is important enough to make you go drinking," interrupted Reba, her touch firmer now. "Nothing is that bad."

Chipper licked his lips and thought of the bottle in his pocket. A desire to justify his actions overcame him, a feeling that he needed to make Reba understand. Though she loved him, she didn't know everything. Fact is, she didn't know a lot. He thought of his stump—Reba didn't know how that stump had come about, didn't know how that moment still haunted him, woke him up at night in cold sweats. He faced her eye to eye, his anger suddenly fueled by both the booze and his need to defend himself.

"You don't know how bad things can get," he said.

Reba nodded slowly. "Maybe you're right," she said. "I don't know all you've experienced, all you've faced."

Instead of appeasing him, her agreement spurred him forward. "You're absolutely right," he said, his tone harsher than he really meant. "You don't know, simple as that. You grew up a banker's daughter, a—

"A bank teller's daughter," she interrupted. "Let's keep it straight."

"Well, you know what I mean." Chipper slipped his hand from hers, stood and leaned over the table, his right hand flat on the wooden top. "You never had no mama die on you when you was just ten, never had to work and scrounge." His face grew red as he spoke and his voice became louder. "Never got sent to no war, never—"

"Keep your voice down!" soothed Reba, a finger over her lips. "I don't want Kyle Lee to hear."

Chipper stopped in mid-sentence, his head swirling,

his heart broken as he thought of his children. A sense of guilt as heavy as a sack of coal pressed down on his shoulders, and his legs quivered. He knew he'd done wrong by buying the liquor. But he hadn't hurt anybody by that. He'd kept his wits about him this time, had bought only one bottle, then come on home, the paycheck intact, the binge unfinished. Didn't Reba see that? Couldn't she at least give him credit for that much?

Wanting to make up with her, he stepped around the table, his right arm extended. Though shaking her head, Reba reached for him too and they came together in the middle of the kitchen, her head on his chest, her hands around his waist.

"I'm sorry," he said, his eyes moist. "But I got this weakness. You know that. It's a pull on me, like the rapids in the creek after a hard rain. It just swooshes me along and I can't seem to fight it, stand up to it."

Reba raised her chin. "I'll fight it with you," she said. "Don't try to do it all alone."

For several long moments, they stood that way, their hearts thumping as one, the smell of flour hanging in the air. But then they heard a baby cry. Andrea Grace had wakened.

Reba patted his sides and gave him another good hug. She froze as if suddenly injected with lead. Her hands had touched the bottle in his jacket. Chipper grabbed her wrist and pulled it from his jacket, his fingers tight on her flesh.

"Is that a liquor bottle?" she asked.

He stared at his feet and nodded his head.

"You brought liquor into this house again?" she asked, her eyes filling. "After all we went through last year? All the promises that you'd never make that mistake again?"

Chipper closed his eyes, the reminder making his shame complete. He'd broken the most important promise of all—that he would never again bring alcohol into the home. A wave of self-hatred worse than anything he'd ever felt washed over him, and he swallowed hard to push back the bile that made him want to throw up.

"You know what happened last time," seethed Reba.

Chipper gritted his teeth. As much as he wanted to forget what had happened, he couldn't. Though too awful to remember, that same awfulness meant he had no power to forget. The memory surged up again . . .

After his binge last December, Chipper had returned home and fallen onto the sofa in a drunken stupor. Kyle Lee had tiptoed in to check on him. Finding a bottle of cheap scotch on the floor by his daddy, Kyle Lee had opened it up and swigged down several swallows. Within minutes he was as drunk as his daddy, stumbling around the room, his little legs wobbly, his eyes glassy.

Chipper dropped Reba's hand and stepped back. This time she let him go.

"I don't know what to say," he said, his defenses in shambles. "I . . ."

"Save it," she said, waving her hands in dismissal. "I don't want to hear it anymore. Too many excuses, too much—"

Desperate to explain, Chipper remembered Ty Bo Shiller.

"Listen to me, Reba," he coaxed. "I went by Ty Bo's.
He . . : his son is coming home. Ty Bo said he had
to—

She raised a hand, palm out, cutting him off before
he could tell her he'd lost his job. "I said I didn't want
to hear it," she said, wiping her eyes on her apron. "I've
heard it for years, all of your excuses. And, Lord knows,
I've tried to understand. But it can't go on any longer.
You blaming your drinking on your missing arm, all
the anger in you coming from that, the anger that
spews out when you get the stuff in your belly, the
depression that always follows your drinking sprees."

She paused to take a breath but he didn't interrupt.
"But you know what, Chipper?" she continued. "I
don't think it's that stump that caused you to take up
drinking. I think it's something deeper than that,
something else the war blasted away. And whatever that
was . . . well, when it was gone, that's when you started
drinking. You've got a hole in your soul—that's your
problem and you've been trying to fill it up ever since
the war with every drop of whiskey you drink."

They stood facing each other now, both of them on
the balls of their feet, tense and ready to pounce. His
heart dropping faster than a dead squirrel from a tree,
Chipper tried to think of a way past the unpleasantness.
But no escape came to him. He dropped his head into
his hand.

"You probably right," he said softly. "There is something missin' in me. But I don't know . . . don't know
what it is . . . don't know how to find it, put it back."

"Well, drinking sure isn't the answer."

An eternity seemed to pass. But then, his eyes watering, Chipper knew what he had to do. Slowly pushing his hand into his pocket, he pulled out the bottle and sat it on the table. The paycheck followed. He handed it to Reba. Silently, she took the check and put it in her apron pocket. Next, she picked up the bottle, untwisted the top, and stepped to the sink. The whiskey gurgled as it disappeared down the drain.

Too ashamed to move, Chipper stood and watched it disappear. From the bedroom, he heard Andrea Grace crying again.

"I need to check on her," said Reba, tossing the empty bottle into the waste basket.

"I still need to tell you something," said Chipper, his hand on her arm.

Reba shivered and eased away from his touch. "What you have to say can wait," she said. "Let's get through Christmas first, then we'll talk about a lot of things."

Her body stiff, she withdrew from the kitchen, the smell of flour disappearing with her. Chipper watched her go, his guilt weighing heavier every second. Reba deserved better, he decided. Better than a man who'd break his promises so easily, a man who used all manner of excuses to explain his unforgivable sins. Her parents were right! He wasn't good enough for Reba!

Chipper's mouth watered, and the desire for a drink came at him harder than a starving dog going after a bone. He thought of the bottle in the trash and, before he could stop himself, leaned down and picked it up.

His tongue as busy as a lizard's, he licked the top of the bottle then tipped it over and drained the last drop from the bottom. All sense of self-respect gone now, he stuck his tongue into the neck and noisily sucked it dry. He heard a door slam. The noise stopped him in mid-lick. For an instant, he stood still, his hand gripping the empty bottle, his heart stricken with the fear of getting caught. A second later his fear turned to even deeper shame and his face flushed. What a loser he was, what a pitiful excuse for a man, lower than dirt on a boot!

Hot with embarrassment, Chipper suddenly knew he couldn't face Reba again right away, couldn't let her see him lso broken and beat up, a lowly creature with no education, no job, no arm, no pride, no hope. As if seeing everything clearly, Chipper instinctively knew he had to leave the house for awhile, had to give Reba time for her anger to subside. He could talk to her later, after she calmed down. He'd lay it all out then, tell her how he'd lost his job. She'd understand then, and with that understanding forgiveness would come. An hour or so should do it, he decided; an hour would clear the air.

Anxious to leave before Reba returned, Chipper tossed the bottle back into the trash and rushed out of the kitchen, zipping his jacket as he walked. From the right, Thumper ran to him, eyes glimmering, tail straight up, a dog on a mission if he ever saw one.

"You want to go with me?" Chipper asked. "Take a little ride?"

Thumper tilted his head as if to question the wisdom of such a trip.

"Suit yourself. I'm goin', either way."

Thumper glanced back at the bedroom toward Reba and Andrea Grace, then faced Chipper once more. He wagged his tail.

"Good," said Chipper, grabbing his hat and opening the door. "We won't be gone long."

With Thumper at his side, Chipper stopped for a second, pivoted back and surveyed the room as if trying to memorize every part of it. From the kids' room he heard Reba singing softly. "Sweet little Jesus boy . . . they made you be born in a manger. Sweet little Jesus boy . . ."

Sighing, Chipper felt an urge to slam the door, rush into the bedroom, and hug Reba so hard she'd almost break. He wanted to promise her once and for all that he'd never fail her or the kids ever again. But, he admitted to himself, he didn't know for sure that he could keep such a promise.

Shoving on his cap, he smelled the Christmas tree one more time, then turned around and closed the door. He rushed through the sleet, climbed into the truck, and started the engine. On the road a few seconds later, he tried to think of a place to go. Not much open at almost seven o'clock on Christmas Eve.

"Stella's is open," he said to Thumper. "You think that's the place?"

The dog whined.

Chipper licked his lips as the urge for a drink again knotted up in his stomach. A man without a job on such a frigid night deserved a drink, he reasoned. No

one could question that. And Reba was already as mad
at him as she could get. One more stick of wood under
it couldn't make a frying pan any hotter. His chin jut-
ting, he pointed the truck toward Stella's Saloon, a
small, smoky bar about six miles out of Asheville.

"About an hour," he said to Thumper. "One drink
and then home for Christmas."

Thumper lay his head by his leg, but didn't speak.
Outside, the sleet seemed to thicken and the wind kept
fighting him for control of the truck. Without warn-
ing, Chipper suddenly hit the brakes, his stump jab-
bing his side. "Money!" he shouted at the sleety night.
"Got no money!"

Thumper raised his head but didn't offer to bankroll
his master, not even a dime. Trying to think of somebody
to loan him a couple of dollars, Chipper eased off the
brakes and the truck moved slowly ahead. But no one
came to mind, nobody he dared to interrupt on Christmas
Eve and ask for money to buy booze. He gritted his teeth.
He needed a drink, just one, to make it through the night.

He pulled the truck over and parked, his mind busy
with options. He considered going back home and
sneaking in the back door. Maybe Reba had taken off
her apron and left it in the kitchen. If so, he'd take his
paycheck, cash it in Asheville, use a couple of dollars
for a drink or two, and then return the rest. But then
he knew he couldn't do that. Reba would kill him if
she caught him. And even if she didn't, he'd never forgive himself for stooping so low as to steal from his
wife. Even as bad as he was, he still hadn't sunk to that

level, at least not yet.

"What you think, Thumper boy?" he asked, more desperate by the moment. "Just a couple of bucks; that's all we need."

Thumper lifted his head, obviously out of ideas. The wind whipped louder around the truck's windows and Chipper heard a slap from the back. Startled, he jerked around, his eyes searching for the source of the noise. He saw the tarp he'd placed over Kyle Lee's bicycle, one end of it loose and flapping in the breeze. "Hold on," he said to Thumper. "Don't want that bike to get scratched up by the sleet."

He jumped out, hopped into the truck bed, and laid the rock back into place. A second later, blowing on his fingers, he rejoined Thumper in the cab.

"Good lookin' bike," he said, patting the dog. "Kyle Lee's gonna love that bicycle."

Thumper pumped his tail against the seat. Though not sure of his destination, Chipper shifted gears and the truck pulled away from the roadside. "Any ideas, boy?" he asked. "Any thoughts?"

Thumper turned away and stared out the window. Chipper blinked and pushed his cap back. As if escaping from the bowels of a slag heap, a monstrous thought suddenly jumped into his head, a notion he knew he should destroy the instant it made its presence known. But try as he might, he couldn't do it. The urge for the drink pulled too strong at his gut, a torment stronger than gravity pulling a child over a cliff on a night without stars. The talons of the monster sank into his flesh and took a hold that nothing could loose. With the sleet pounding above him like a thousand roofers nailing down shingles, Chipper Gaines made a decision to do something that even the most corrupt of men might hesitate to do, much less the loving father of a precious son. But, pulled along into the evil that even good men sometimes do when tempted by vile things, he decided to do it anyway.

3

PIECES OF SILVER

The sign that blinked at Chipper had three bulbs missing, but he pulled his truck to a halt in the muddy driveway and paid no attention. Hoping against hope that the establishment was still open, he hopped out, left Thumper in the cab, and hustled to the front door. A thin light seeped from the seedy building and lit Chipper's gaunt face with a ghoulish glare. A shudder in his shoulders, he rapped on the door. No one answered. The wind jerked a sapling tree almost parallel to the ground, its boughs stretched out as if trying to reach Chipper. He involuntarily drew closer to the door and knocked again, harder. The knuckle on his index finger cracked and started to bleed. As he wiped it on his jeans, he heard movement from inside the building.

"Who's there?" The voice sounded gruff.

"Chipper Gaines. That you, Billy?"

"It sure ain't the King of England. Who else gonna be here at seven the p.m. on Christmas Eve?" The door creaked open, and a skinny man at least seventy years old with an Adam's apple the size of a grapefruit stood in the entrance, his thin fingers hooked under a set of black suspenders. "What you doin' here, Gaines?" He stepped back to let Chipper enter. A cigarette dangled from between a pair of fingers yellowed by nicotine.

"Need a deal," said Chipper, his eyes busy over the interior of the small shop, but landing nowhere in particular. Crowded by every imaginable kind of item—used sofa cushions, pictures stacked on top of each other, enough watches to put two on the arm of everyone in Buckview—and everything in between—the place smelled like stale cigarettes. Chipper saw an ashtray on the counter by the cash register. A curl of weak smoke climbed up out of the ashes. Chipper rubbed his nose.

"I'm a deal maker," said Billy, fingers back in his suspenders as he stepped behind the counter. "What you got for me?"

"In the truck," Chipper said, studying his brogans. "Got it in the truck."

"Well, I ain't goin' out in this foul weather to fetch it."

Chipper looked up as if surprised. "Hey, yeah, sure, let me get it."

"Now there's an idea." Billy perched himself on a stool behind the counter, his thin white hair sprigging out in all directions, and pulled a new cigarette from his shirt pocket.

Chipper nodded and rushed back out, his mind

jumbled. Ignoring the sleet that tapped on his head, he ran to the truck, paused, took a breath and licked his lips. He saw Thumper staring at him through the back window of the cab.

"Just for tonight," Chipper whispered into the wind. "Cash the check tomorrow, buy it back the day after Christmas."

Thumper's head slipped down so that only his ears and neck were visible.

"He's getting a baseball, too," he continued to protest. "And shirts and jeans. Enough candy to make him sick for a week. The boy's spoiled already."

Thumper dropped completely out of sight with a thin whine.

Moving quickly to keep from changing his mind, Chipper hopped into the truck bed, lifted the rocks from the canvas, and pulled it back. The red bicycle lay there in all its splendor, dry and sparkling, its shiny paint fresh and unscathed. Chipper stood over it for several seconds, his eyes fixed as if staring at a light in a tunnel with a train at the other end.

"Leave it," said a voice in his head. "Take the bike, and go home."

"A drink," said a second voice. "Just one drink. Nothin' to it. Cash your check and reclaim the bike on Monday. Billy won't do nothing with it 'till you come back. Give Kyle Lee the bike on January 25, that's his birthday and you got nothin' for him for that . . . and with no job you got no way to buy him anything between now and then. One drink—it'll help you tell

Reba you lost your job."

He heard a door open, looked up and saw Billy on the steps of his shop, a cigarette smoldering in his fingers.

"I ain't plannin' to wait here all night on you," Billy yelled. "You comin' or what?"

"Hold your water," Chipper shouted. "Be right there."

He faced the bike once more and licked his lips. His mouth watered. He needed a drink badly. Kyle Lee had a baseball under the tree. No need for a bicycle, too. He'd give him the bike for his birthday.

His hands shaking, Chipper grabbed the tarp and pulled it completely off the bike. "One drink," said one voice.

"Go home to Reba," said another.

"One drink."

"Go home."

He grabbed the bike by the handlebars, hooked his stump under the back wheel, and hauled it out of the truck. Then, moving like a man running from an angry bear, he hustled across the yard and into Billy's shop. Sitting the bike down, he pushed it over to Billy.

"Purty bike you got there'," said Billy, examining the bicycle. "Looks to be brand new."

"It is that," said Chipper, proud in spite of what he planned to do. "Been payin' layaway on her."

"I'm bettin' somebody's expecting that bike for Christmas."

Chipper dropped his eyes for a second. In Buckview, everybody knew everybody. Even though he didn't do regular business with Billy Johnson, the man had no doubt figured out this bike was set to go to Kyle Lee for Christmas. But what business was it of his? Yeah, Billy knew Reba and the kids because he was a deacon down at the church, but that didn't give him the right to stick his nose in on something like this.

His jaw set, Chipper faced Billy again. He had his fingers in his suspenders. A half-smoked cigarette dangled from his lips.

"That's not your concern, far as I can tell," Chipper said evenly. "You interested or not?"

Billy puffed his cigarette, walked around the bike, and scrutinized it from stem to stern. "No scratches on her, no dirt neither. She's clean all right." He dropped the cigarette to the concrete floor, and stomped it out with his black shoe. "What you want for her?"

Chipper licked his lips. "Maybe twenty dollars," he said.

Billy grunted. "That's about what you paid for her, I reckon," he said. "Give you eight."

"Oh, come on now Billy," said Chipper. "Everybody says you're tight enough to squeeze a dime and make her squeak, but nobody ever called you a thief. You gotta give me seventeen, not a nickel less. That's a fair price, and I'm coming back in here Monday to pick this beauty right back up. You just holdin' her for a day, no more."

Billy snapped a suspender, walked around the bike again. "Ten," he said. "That's about half of what you paid."

Chipper studied the man for several seconds. He

didn't know him well, but he had a reputation as a fair man, even if he did keep the most cluttered shop in the history of Buckview. He knew ten wasn't right and so did Billy.

"Fourteen," Chipper argued. "Fourteen is reasonable for both of us. And it's only for a day."

Billy popped a suspender. "You drive a hard bargain, boy," he said. "But since you got a wife sweeter than a peppermint stick and two of the purtiest kids I ever set eyes on, I'll give you twelve and fifty cents. And if you don't take that, you can push that red bike back out into that sleet and drive it on away from here." He stopped and snapped a suspender.

Chipper rubbed his hand over the bicycle seat. He knew enough to know that if he tried to squeeze Billy any further he'd likely drop his offer. "Done," he said. "But only for a day. Be back on Monday to claim this baby."

Billy pulled out a fresh cigarette, lit it, and took a drag. "You sure you want to do this?" he asked, smoke spewing from his nostrils. "This bike looks 'bout the right size for Kyle Lee."

Chipper paused, his heart at war with itself. The last chance to do the right thing stared him in the face. He thought of Kyle Lee. The boy didn't know for sure that he even had a bicycle. And he did need something to give him on his birthday. But he had no job. "I want to do it," he said. "Got my reason. . . . And I'm buyin' it back before you can even put it in the window."

Billy kicked the front wheel. "She is a looker," he

said. "Be easy to sell this one."

"Don't you even think of sellin' her before you talk to me."

"Fair enough. Somebody want this bike, I talk to you first."

"You got it."

Billy pulled a wad of bills from his pants, counted out twelve one-dollar bills, handed the stack and five dimes to Chipper, and stuck the rest back in his pocket. Chipper shoved the money into his jacket, rubbed the bicycle one last time, and pushed it over to Billy. Without another word, the skinny man grabbed the handlebars and rolled the bike toward the back of the counter, his cigarette dropping a trail of ashes as he walked away.

Chipper pivoted and skulked out, his shoulders hunched, his head down. At the door, he stopped for a second and turned around. Billy and the bike had disappeared into a back room. Telling himself that he'd come back on Monday with the money to reclaim the gift, Chipper rushed to the truck. Beside Thumper again, he patted the dog on the head and drove away from Billy's Pawn Shop, the last three letters in the word "P-A-W-N" as lifeless and dull as the feeling he had in the pit of his gut.

4

WARNINGS

It didn't take Chipper long to wash his guilt into near-drunkenness. A quick drive to Stella's Saloon, a roadside honky-tonk with peeling paint and no screen door; a hurried run to the door, with Thumper left in the truck; a sit-down at a well-polished, darkly-stained maple bar that gave solid evidence that Stella spent more money on the inside than on the outside of her establishment. Not one drink but four, one shot of cheap whiskey after another from a clear glass that sparkled in the dim light of the room. Chipper took the liquor straight, no ice—guzzle, guzzle, guzzle—his hand shaky as he slugged down the warm liquid.

After the fourth drink, his hand finally stopped shaking, and he took a breath long enough to stare around and see if he knew anybody. Nope, not a soul. Just three other people in the room, two not counting Stella, the bartender. He faced Stella once more. Having gone a year without a drink, the alcohol was working quickly into his system.

"One fuh the rrroad, Stella," he said, his speech slightly slurred.

"You sure you okay to drive?" asked Stella, a wide woman with gray hair pinned back in a tidy bun and a stomach as round as a washtub.

Chipper waved off her concern. "I hold my drink," he said, concentrating to speak clearly. "Better than most. You know that."

Stella shrugged and poured him another drink.

"What time you closin' tonight?" asked Chipper, anxious to make conversation and show Stella he wasn't drunk.

"Oh, midnight or so. Based on who comes in."

"Good," said Chipper, laying the remainder of his money on the stool beside him and counting out the cash for the fifth drink. "You deserve to go . . . go home for Chris . . ." he had trouble pronouncing the word. "Chris . . . mas."

"You need to move it on home yourself," said Stella, wiping her thick hands on the apron that struggled to cover her girth. "Weather's worse by the minute."

Blinking, Chipper thought about what she'd said. The roads were getting slick. And he did have some awful bad tires. Maybe he should head back to Reba, even as much as he dreaded telling her about Ty Bo. "Okay," he said, slugging down the drink. "Home it is."

Stella nodded and picked up his empty glass. Chipper stood, zipped up his jacket, waved to Stella and headed to the door. Outside, the sleet seemed to have increased its intensity. It was now a driving sheet of white ice clicking and clacking like glass shattering. Numbed by the scotch, Chipper hardly noticed. His hat pushed back, he moved to the truck, stepped unsteadily inside, and plopped down. Thumper whined, poked Chipper's hand with his nose, then turned and faced toward home.

Chipper patted the dog's back. "Lesss go . . . go home," he slurred, his eyes suddenly tired. "Home . . . be warm at home."

Thumper wagged his tail, and Chipper stuck the key in the ignition. Seconds later the truck pulled out of the driveway, its thin lights peering through the sleet like pin pricks against a black blanket. Bending low over the steering wheel, Chipper squinted through the frigid darkness, his hand cold on the wheel, his stump squeezed against his side.

The road twisted down and to the left, or at least what he could still see of the road. The sleet had covered most of it in white. Gaining speed on the downward incline, Chipper touched the brakes to slow the truck down. But instead of losing speed, it seemed to increase even more. He pressed the brakes harder. The truck started to slide, its wheels locking on the frozen road. A gust of wind grabbed the back of the truck and pulled it to the left. Chipper eased off the brakes to stop the slide, but the wheels refused to cooperate. The machine seemed to take on a mind of its own, and the hood slid toward the road's edge.

Suddenly alert, Chipper jerked the wheel to the right and hit the gas again, thinking he'd speed the truck out of its skid.

The cab jumped forward, a rusty block of metal fired at the bottom of the grade like a cannonball from a gun. From the right, Chipper saw a huge shadow dart into the road, a black apparition wearing a cape as wide as a garage door. But then the cape formed up and became a man, a black-faced man dressed in rags, his fingers poking through the ends of a pair of black gloves, his toothless face staring at Chipper like grim death. The hands were huge—the fingers seeming like the prongs of a pitchfork—and they were raised toward Chipper, palms out as if the man thought he could stop the oncoming truck by the mere act of extending his arms.

His heart in his throat, Chipper whipped the steering wheel to the right and the truck burrowed through the night, ramming toward a stand of evergreens on the side of the road. For a second Chipper thought he'd missed the man, and he almost started to breath again. But then he heard a sickening thump and realized that the truck's left fender had clipped the apparition. The black man rolled up the fender toward the windshield, his cape fanning out like a buzzard's wings, momentarily blocking Chipper's view. Chipper heard Thumper barking, but the sound seemed far away, and he kept his eyes fixed straight ahead. The cape flew up and over the windshield and disappeared over the back, and the black man dropped out of sight.

The truck raked down and through the trees, the boughs of pines, laurels, and maples scratching the sides. Faster and faster went the truck as the hill dropped, gathering force all the way. Steering as much as possible, Chipper dodged the largest of the trees and somehow the truck never hit anything head on. Ten seconds after leaving the road, it jerked to a stop. Chipper's head banged against the steering wheel, and a bump the size of a walnut swelled up immediately over his right eye. Groaning, he grabbed his head and glanced over at Thumper. The dog had skidded from the seat onto the floorboard, but he quickly jumped up by Chipper and licked his face. He was fine.

Though groggy, Chipper hugged the dog as hard as he could. "You're okay, boy!" he whispered breathlessly. "You're okay!"

His body shaking, Thumper whoofed and licked Chipper's chin. Something bumped the truck from the back, and Chipper suddenly remembered the man!

Shutting off the engine, he grabbed the door handle and stumbled out, his eyes searching. Remarkably, the wind suddenly died, and the sleet likewise quickly eased away. Chipper heard a grunt from the right and stepped toward it. His head began to spin as he moved, and a second later it started to pound—he felt something wet over his right eye. His fingers touched the wetness and he realized he was bleeding. Woozy, he sagged back against the truck fender.

"I be over here!" The voice rolled through the dark like the foghorn from a lighthouse. Chipper felt shivers run up his spine.

"I can't see you," he shouted, trying to stay focused.

"Keep talkin'."

"You the one needs to keep talkin'," boomed the black man. "I finds my way to you."

"You okay?" yelled Chipper, remembering the thud of flesh and bone against the truck.

"I be fine," yelled the man. "Sore in the hip maybe tomorrow." He sounded closer now. "But nothin' a body cain't forget in a few hours. You?"

Chipper touched the cut over his eye. It was still bleeding. He pressed his palm into it to slow the flow. The apparition suddenly stood beside him, no more than four feet away. His vision blurred, but Chipper pulled himself erect and peered out at a black man standing at least six and a half feet tall and at least sixty years old, maybe more. He had a face with more lines than a treeless hillside after a hard rain and eyes the color of used motor oil. A touch of fear rippled through Chipper's feet. If this man felt unkindly toward him for running him over, he'd have a hard time defending himself in his current condition. Thankfully, though, the man made no threatening move.

Chipper's vision steadied. The cape on the black man's shoulders was tattered. He wore a gray sweater of equal wear under the cape and pants only slightly darker and no less frayed. Strangely, though, his boots looked good . . . almost new—only a scuff or two on the toes gave evidence of any use. Out of the darkness, Thumper appeared, his nose at Chipper's knees.

"You sure you okay?" asked Chipper, ignoring his

dog and examining the man from head to toe.

"I'm fine. You just grazed me some. Not even no blood on me. You want to see?"

Before he could answer, the man did a slow turn, his long arms extended, his cape hovering in the air as wide as a drape. Facing Chipper again, he dropped his arms.

"Now we best give you the inspection," he said, walking closer. "See what hurts done come upon you." No more than a foot away, the man towered over Chipper. He took his palm from the cut on his forehead. The black man leaned over to see.

"You got a right smart bump on yo noggin'," said the man, touching Chipper's forehead. "Bleedin', too." He ran his fingers over the wound. "Bet you feelin' a touch faint, maybe got a throbbin' in your head, too." He stepped back. "You might need to see yoself a doctor."

"I'll be okay," said Chipper, though not as sure as he sounded. "Just need to get home."

The black man shrugged. "Home be good," he said. "But maybe see a doctor, too. Yo thank your truck be all right?" He nodded toward the headlights still flooding the area.

"Yeah, think so."

"Then maybe we oughta try drivin' it outta here."

Chipper nodded as if everything was clear as glass. But the fact of the matter was that he was greatly confused, and it wasn't all because of the pain behind his eyes. Who was this huge man? And what was he doing out on such a bad night, and Christmas Eve to boot?

Though he wanted a few questions answered before he climbed into his truck with the stranger, Chipper knew he had no right to ask the man anything. He'd just about killed him, so he at least owed him a ride, no questions asked!

Tightening his cap, Chipper nodded and headed to the truck. The man followed.

"You got a name?" Chipper asked, his hand on the truck door.

"Most folks just call me Mose."

"I'm Bailey Gaines, but folks call me Chipper." He lifted a foot to climb up. But a quick rush of the woozies ran over him again, and his foot slipped off the sideboard. He sagged down, his face against the cold metal of the truck door.

"Hold on there, Mr. Chipper," said Mose, rushing around to him. "You maybe hurt worser than we thought." Slipping his big hands under Chipper's arms, he heaved him up, opened the passenger door, and pushed him onto the seat. Slamming the door, he scrambled back the other way, opened the door, motioned Thumper in, grabbed Chipper by the biceps, and slid him over to the passenger side. Shutting the door, he moved to the driver's side again and climbed in. Chipper lay on the cold seat, his eyes staring at the dashboard, his head throbbing. Touching the bump on his head, he groaned in pain.

"Gotta go . . . go home," he mumbled, trying but failing to raise up. "My wife will be wondering where I am.""

"I be tryin'," said Mose, closing the door and punching the ignition. "Just soon as I get this machine runnin' and you point me in the right way." The engine caught and held. Mose stuck it in reverse and hit the gas. The wheels spun in the mud, throwing up big chunks of pine straw mixed with mountain soil and sleet. He eased off the gas for a second, then hit it again. The truck rocked backward and inched a foot or so up the hill, but then stopped again, stuck in place. Mose revved the engine for several more seconds but nothing else happened, and he let off the gas.

"She mired down," he said, slipping the gears to neutral. "Seems we gonna need somebody to do some pushin'." He stared over at Chipper. Chipper tried to focus on the button on the glove compartment.

"You think you up to drivin'?" Mose asked. "Let me throw a shoulder under that right wheel?"

Chipper tried to nod but couldn't move his head. The dashboard twisted around and around, the button on the glove compartment spinning like a wheel in a clockwise motion. Chipper felt a hand on his face and realized Mose was checking the knot on his head again. A second later, he heard Mose turn off the engine. He felt a whoosh of frigid air, heard a door slam. He bit his lip and knew that Mose had left.

Okay. Though cold and lonely, he certainly understood. No reason for Mose to stay behind and worry about him. No doubt the black man wanted to move on to wherever it was he needed to go. Chipper curled into a fetal position and closed his eyes. A short nap, he thought, then home.

The door on his side creaked open. His eyes blinked. A shadow moved toward his face. He opened his mouth to call out for help! Something cold and wet pressed down on his forehead and over his eyes. He jerked away. A deep bass voice eased through the black night.

"It's Mose," said the voice. "Just puttin' ice on yo hurt. Stay easy, easy."

Unable to fight any longer, Chipper immediately relaxed, his body sagging. The ice, wrapped up in a black rag, ached his face for a few seconds, then numbed it to the point he no longer felt anything. From a distance he heard his door slam and the one on the driver's side open. He felt Mose move, and he opened his eyes and watched in wonder as the black man took off his cape and brushed ice off the shoulders.

"This maybe warms you up some," said Mose, laying the cape over Chipper's upper body. "Make you all toasty."

Though he wanted to protest against the man's kindness, Chipper knew it would do no good; so he just mumbled "thanks" and closed his eyes once more.

"We wait us a while," said Mose. "Give you some time to catch yo breath."

"You're mighty nice to me," Chipper said. "I'm thanking you for it."

Mose shrugged. "People ought to be nice," he said. "World be a whole lot better place iffen they would."

Silence lay on the truck for several minutes. The

wind outside started moving again, and Thumper
whined. Chipper's thoughts drifted . . . Reba, Kyle Lee,
Andrea Grace, the bicycle, the booze. Guilt seeped in,
then the war . . . the day. . . . Shaking his head he
forced away the thoughts and made himself concen-
trate on the present situation. His mind began to clear
some.

"You from around here?" he asked Mose, opening
his eyes. "Don't know that I ever saw you in
Buckview."

Mose smiled. "Used to be, long time ago. Still got
family over by Asheville."

"That where you headed?"

"Yeh, thought I'd peek in on 'em for Christmas."

"You walking?"

Moses touched the steering wheel, ran his fingers
over it. "Walkin' some. Hobo on a train some. Peoples
give me a ride time to time. You know, heah and there,
I makes it where I needs to go."

Chipper nodded and silence came again. He
thought about Reba, knew she'd be worried sick. He
tried to push up, but his head still wouldn't cooperate.
He lay back down.

Mose broke the silence this time. "I knows it ain't
my place to go pryin'," he started. "But what's a man
like you doin' out on Christmas Eve? Ain't nothin'
open this time a night."

Chipper's face flushed in the dark, and he wished he
didn't have to answer. But then he thought, why not,
what difference did it make? After tonight, he'd never

see Mose again. Besides, he realized as he considered it, he needed to tell somebody, wanted to talk about a thing or two. And Mose seemed so calm—almost as if he'd seen and heard so much in his life that nothing could surprise or shock him anymore.

"I went out for a Christmas drink," Chipper said, keeping it simple.

"I thought I smelt it," said Mose, without accusation. "More'n one, I 'spect."

Chipper grunted. "You're right about that," he said. "Too much."

Moses rubbed his chin. Outside, the wind swirled a bit faster, and the sleet started to fall again. "Man drinkin' a lot on Christmas Eve must have a bunch on his mind," he said.

"More than I want, that's for sure."

"You wanna talk about it?"

Chipper sighed and wished he had the courage to say it all, to uncover everything that chewed away at his soul. But he didn't, and he knew it. So he decided he'd said enough. "Maybe not ready for that," he said.

"Suit yourself." Moses said, laying his hands back on the wheel. "Man be ready when he's ready, not until."

The sleet hammered on the roof now, and the wind keened. Moses continued. "But I needs to say one thing to you, iffen you don't mind."

"It's a free country."

Mose faced him now, his long face calm but firm. Even in the dark, his eyes were bright. His voice seemed to deepen even more as he raised it to speak over the weather. His tones seemed to rise right from the core of the earth, rich and full, and juiced with power.

"I's once a drinkin' man, too," he rumbled. "Drinkin', drinkin', drinkin', all da time. Oh, I had my reasons, mind you, good ones, too." He stared into Chipper's eyes and Chipper wanted to turn away, but he found himself unable. He felt mesmerized by the black man—his voice and eyes, the eyes that seemed to see right into the interior of his brain, into the dark places of his mind where awful things hid, the awful things from the past, from the war, from the day he lost his arm, the day he . . .

Chipper pushed away the memory and focused on Mose as he kept talking, almost shouting now. "But all those good reasons for drinkin' didn't hep me nary a bit there at the end, there when the drinkin' finally took me over for good." Mose stopped and stared past Chipper into the black night.

"What happened?" asked Chipper, sitting up before he knew it. "What happened to you?"

"I losted everything," wailed Mose. "Job, wife, babies—six of 'em—all gone, everything. I ended up on the road, no home, no family, losted all I loved, life itself . . . "

Chipper wanted to ask more questions, but Mose kept talking, giving him no chance to interrupt.

"Look at me!" Mose shouted. "Take yourself a long hard look!" He opened his arms to offer a good view— the gloves without fingers, the tattered clothing, the weary lines in the face. "You lookin' at your future, Mr. Chipper Gaines! Your future! Here it is . . . you be all by yourself, wanderin' the roads on Christmas Eve, nothin' and nobody but you! This is it! All that's out there for the rest of your natural born days iffen you don't straighten out. This is it, Mr. Chipper Gaines, this is it!"

A limb broke off a tree outside and slammed into the top of the cab. Chipper jerked back against the seat, and Thumper jumped up beside him. Chipper hugged his dog and breathed rapidly, his mind as tossed as the limb in the wind. As if worn out by the speech, Mose suddenly dropped his arms and slumped over, head on chest. Outside, the wind calmed too and the sleet tapered off.

Trying to relax, Chipper patted Thumper and told his heart to settle. What Mose said scared him more than he wanted to admit. But he didn't know if he could do anything about it. Maybe he was destined to end up like Mose, alone and penniless, a drifter with nothing and no one. But he didn't want it to happen. He reached over and touched Mose on the arm. The black man looked up at him.

"I did a mighty bad thing tonight," Chipper said, thinking of the bicycle. "About as bad a thing as a man can do."

"Don't surprise me none to hear you say that," said Mose. "You got the look of the guilt on you."

"I got this pull on me, the drive to drink, but I had no money."

"Liquor make a strong man go weak in the knees," agreed Mose. "I knows how it is. I once stole money my baby girl made from doin' wash for a white woman. Liquor makes a man low down, that be for sure."

"I . . . I . . ." Chipper wanted to say it out loud, to tell Mose that he had matched his foul act, that he had hocked his boy's Christmas bike. He wanted to say it straight out, hold the awful thing up so somebody else but him could look at it, see how mean it was. But his pride wouldn't let him do it, not here, not to a stranger, not even one as kind as Mose.

Mose touched his hand. "I maybe not the one you needs to tell," he said. "Maybe you needs to tell the ones closest to you, the ones most touched by what you did or didn't."

Chipper nodded and thought of his family. He wanted to see them immediately, wanted to go home and confess, go home and hug Reba and the kids, hug them until they hurt from it.

"I think I might can drive now," he said, his voice energized. "Let's see if we can move this truck."

Mose gazed at him without moving. Though puzzled, Chipper handed him his cape. "Thanks for this," he said. "You've been a help. We get this truck on the road, I'll swing by my house, tell my missus I'm okay, then I'll take you where you want to go. That okay?"

"You hear what I said, Mr. Chipper?" Mose asked. "What I said 'bout your future?"

"I heard," said Chipper, eyes on the dashboard.

"I heard."

Hauling in a deep breath, Mose slipped the cape over his shoulders. "I think you be a good man," he said, opening the door. "But maybe you forgets how to feel that goodness, don't know anymore what to do with it. I'm tellin' you maybe you need to let it out again; it won't hurt you none."

Chipper started to respond; but Mose had already moved away, the door shut behind him. He saw the man move to the driver's-side front fender and spread his feet to catch traction. Moving quickly, Chipper slid under the wheel and flipped on the engine and lights. Peering through the windshield, he saw Moses by the stuck wheel. The sleet had stopped. He rolled down his window.

"I ready, Mr. Chipper," yelled Mose. "I count three, then you romp her down. We make her move, you just see."

Chipper grinned slightly and revved up the engine.

"One, two . . ." Mose twisted sideways, threw his right shoulder against the truck, and grabbed the bumper. "Three." He heaved his shoulder under the fender and Chipper saw a white patch flash on his cape—a patch with a strange emblem on it, an emblem that looked vaguely familiar, but one he couldn't identify in that quick moment.

"Gun it, Mr. Chipper!" yelled Mose.

Forgetting the patch, Chipper hit the gas harder and Mose grunted. The truck rocked, rocked, rocked, and the wheels caught. The truck darted back and up through the woods with a whoosh of rapid movement. Leaving Mose behind, the truck rolled back up the way it had come, its sides taking a beating again. Seconds later, the back wheels bounced back onto the road, and Chipper hit the brakes and slammed to a stop.

"We did it!" he yelled to Thumper. "Drove this baby right out of there!"

His head out the window, Chipper breathed deeply and waited for Mose to appear from below the slope. But the black man didn't come. Confused, Chipper listened for several more seconds. But he heard nothing.

"Hey, Mose!" he yelled. "You okay?" Only the wind answered.

Worried that Mose might be hurt, Chipper grabbed a flashlight from under the seat, hopped out of the truck, and then walked to the edge of the road and looked below.

"Mose!" he shouted, training the light down the hill. "You okay?" There was no response.

Balancing himself by holding to a succession of tree branches, he eased back down the slope, his feet slipping and sliding but his head staying clear. At the bottom of the incline, he found the spot where the truck had been stuck, saw the ruts where the wheels had dug into the ground. But he saw no sign of Mose.

Thumper appeared from nowhere, his nose working the ground. The flashlight busy, Chipper searched the entire area—behind every rock, tree, and bush. But the effort came up empty. No Mose anywhere, not even a set of footprints leading off into the dark.

Confused, Chipper stopped and scratched Thumper behind the ears. "Where'd he go, boy?" he asked.

Thumper whined.

"Mose!" Chipper shouted. "You still here?" He heard nothing, not even the wind.

"You think I need to report it?" he asked Thumper. "Go to the police?"

Thumper whined again.

After raking the flashlight over the area once more and calling out several more times, Chipper shook his head, pushed his cap down over his eyes, and climbed back up the hill. In the truck, he waited a few more minutes to see if Mose might appear. But then, when nothing happened, he patted Thumper on the head and pointed the truck toward home.

5

BIRDS OF A FEATHER

The house was dark. Thumper at his side, Chipper ran toward the front door, his heart pounding. Pushing inside, he flipped on a light and stood in the front room, his cap in hand.

"Reba!" he shouted. "Kyle Lee!" Though he continued to call out as he checked the two bedrooms, he already knew they weren't home. Puzzled, he stepped back to the front room and held his hand over the heater. The stove was almost cold. No one had fed it any wood for at least an hour.

Thumper leading the way, Chipper moved to the kitchen and hit a light switch. Four empty plates sat expectantly in their places on the table. Chipper pulled open the refrigerator. A finished apple pie sat on the top shelf. Chipper shoved his cap back on.

"She left me," he said softly.

Thumper whined, his ears sagging in harmony with his master's mood. Utterly defeated, Chipper sat down, his head in his hand. The knot on his forehead hurt as he touched it, and the floor tile quivered before his eyes. He wondered if he still had alcohol in his bloodstream. Or had the bump caused the floor to move?

Thumper lay down by his feet. For several minutes, neither of them moved. Chipper's mind reeled. He'd lost his job, pawned his son's bike, run over a man. Now this—Reba and the kids were gone, maybe for good. But where? And how? She had no car.

He stood and rubbed his chin and knew immediately that Reba had run to her folks in Asheville. Where else? The Fullers would take her in, no questions asked. Reba had probably walked the quarter mile to the nearest neighbor and called her parents from there. They'd have driven from Asheville to pick her up. She was probably there now, sitting by a fireplace, Kyle Lee and Andrea Grace already in bed. Her parents were no doubt crying over her while sharing sly looks with one another—looks that said they it knew all along. A wash of grief hit Chipper. Separated from his wife and kids on Christmas Eve, maybe for ev—

He pushed away the depressing notion. As he did a rush of anger momentarily replaced his grief. A whole host of perceived slights banged around in his head. Her parents had no right to dislike him. He'd treated their daughter with love and respect. But they still seemed to see him as an outsider. The urge for a drink welled up in his throat, but he fought it back. No matter how angry he felt, he didn't want that now, didn't need it! Liquor had never done anything good for him, anything at all!

Fighting the compulsion, he left the kitchen and headed to the truck, Thumper with him. He'd call Reba, he decided, tell her everything that had happened, confess the awful thing with the bike. He'd promise Reba he'd stay straight this time, tell her he wanted to come pick her up, bring her home for Christmas, home where she belonged.

In the truck, he started it and stared at Thumper. "Who's got a phone?" he asked. Thumper's only response was a blank stare.

Chipper thought of their neighbors but decided he shouldn't interrupt them on Christmas Eve. He rubbed his chin. Only one place he knew open. But he hated the thought of going back to the bar. Too much temptation lurking there.

"Maybe I should just drive on over to the Fullers' place," he mumbled. But he feared that might lead to a disaster. True, Reba had a long fuse; but when it blew, she stayed hot for a good long spell. He shuddered at the possibilities if he showed up without her permission and she hadn't cooled down yet.

"I'll just use the phone," he said to Thumper. "Into Stella's for a jiffy, then out. Okay?"

Thumper popped the seat with his tail, obviously pleased.

Chipper pointed the truck toward the bar. Outside, the sleet started to fall again, this time mixed with snow. The truck slipped and slid on the road as he drove, but he didn't slow down. Though focused on his driving, Chipper also rehearsed what he'd say to Reba when he reached her, how he'd convince her to give him one more chance. He'd tell her about Mose, about how the man had shown him he needed to change. Feeling hopeful, he covered the remaining distance to the bar and pulled up outside. Leaving Thumper, he hugged his jacket closer and hustled inside. A wave of warmth hit him as he entered, and he unzipped the jacket. A song crooned out from the jukebox, and he recognized the voice of Bing Crosby.

"I'm dreaming tonight of a place I love," sang Crosby. "Even more than I usually do. And although it's a long road back . . . I promise you. I'll be home for Christmas . . ."

Grunting, Chipper bellied up to the bar and glanced quickly around, looking for Stella. A young man in a brown suit, a starched white shirt, and a crisp, black fedora that hung low over his eyes, sat alone near the end of the bar. Chipper stepped to the man.

"Where's Stella?" he asked.

The man pushed back the hat, revealing a face no older than Chipper's, and a set of eyes bluer than a robin's eggs.

"Stella stepped to the rear of the building," said the man, his diction clean and precise.

Chipper studied the man for a second, then stepped past him to a doorway behind the bar. "Hey, Stella!" he called. "I use your phone?"

A second later, Stella appeared from the back room, a towel in her hands. "You back here already?" she asked. "Reba not gone be happy with you."

Chipper shrugged. "Don't need no lecture Stella, just a phone."

"Ty Bo Shiller come lookin' for you a while ago," she said.

"He say what he wanted?" asked Chipper, slightly angry.

"Nope—just said if you come back, to let him know."

"Don't need you doin' that," said Chipper. "My business is my business."

Stella lay the towel on the bar and studied him closely. "That's some bump on your noggin," she said, polishing the bar. "Everything all right?"

Chipper licked his lips. "Hard night," he said. "Maybe I'll tell you about it sometime."

"Bartenders listen good," said Stella. "Got nothin' else to do. Phone's back there." She nodded toward the room behind the bar. "Help yourself."

Moving past her, Chipper entered Stella's tiny office and saw the phone hanging on the wall by a small wooden desk. He rang up the operator and gave her the number. His heart thumping, he tried to figure how to start the conversation. Fifteen seconds later, the operator came back. "I'm having a problem with that number," she said. "Hold on and I'll try it again."

Chipper sat down on the corner of Stella's desk and brushed his fingers across the top. The operator came back on the phone. "Those lines are down," she said. "Lots of sleet and snow in Asheville tonight. You'll need to try again later."

"How long before they fix the lines?"

The operator chuckled. "When the sleet stops, I guess."

Stunned, Chipper hung up and sagged against the wall. He hadn't anticipated this. Shoulders slumped, he left the phone and headed back to the bar. Stella met him at the door, her towel over her shoulder. "You make your call?" she asked.

Chipper shook his head and plopped down on a stool. Crosby's smooth voice seemed to mock him as the song from the juke box wound down.

"I'll be home for Christmas . . . You can count on me. . . "

"Lines are all down," Chipper mumbled. "No calls going through to Asheville."

Stella nodded. "I hear they maybe closin' the road, too. Nothin' but emergencies going between here and Asheville tonight. You want some coffee?"

His mind on Reba, Chipper waved Stella away. He hoped Reba and her folks had made it through before the roads shut down. He couldn't bear the thought of his family sitting cold on the highway somewhere.

Stella moved off, her wide frame headed to a table that needed cleaning. Chipper lay his head down and stared into the mirror that wrapped around the back wall of the six-stool bar. His reflection came back at him, haggard and haunted. He made a fist, lay his chin on it, and studied himself. A twenty-seven-year old war veteran with a wife and two kids, a third on the way. Nothing wrong with that. He studied his face some

more, reflecting on the downside of the picture. He
had less education than a circus monkey, no job anywhere on the horizon, a wife who didn't want him,
and a taste for booze that rivaled a pig's love for slop.

In spite of the cozy feel of the bar, a sense of loneliness ran deeply though him. He thought of his family
waking up on Christmas morning without him, and
his breath caught as he felt the deep sorrow well up
from his gut. Kyle Lee would ask Reba about him,
want to know why he wasn't there. Reba wouldn't lie
of course. She'd say something like, "Daddy had something to take care of," or "Daddy wants to be here but
had some pressing business."

His youthful curiosity tempered by a vague unease,
Kyle Lee would want to question her further but
wouldn't. He'd remember that his daddy had disappeared like this at other times in his life—that he'd
stayed away for a few days, then turned back up again.
He'd know that his daddy had a tendency to act like
Thumper sometimes did, to run off for a few nights of
sport and then come home, his head hung in shame,
his body weary and ready to sleep.

Dejected, Chipper lifted his head off his fist. A wave
of dizziness hit him, and a dull ache rose up from
behind his eyes. He rubbed the bump on his forehead.
It seemed to have swelled in the last few minutes. He
rubbed his eyes and tried to push away the guilt that
tugged at his guts. He'd make it better, he promised
himself, as soon as the weather cleared and he could
talk to Reba.

Stella waddled back to the bar and poured the man in the fedora a drink from a bottle of scotch. Her towel busy, Stella moved to Chipper.

"You need anything?" she asked.

Chipper sighed and stared around the bar. A fireplace burned on the opposite wall. A Christmas tree sat in the corner, a string of colored lights blinking off and on, off and on. All in all, the place felt pretty good. He remembered his house, how empty it felt only a few minutes ago. He thought of Reba again and hated that he had no way to contact her, no way to drive to Asheville. Seeing no better option, he decided he might as well stay put until Stella closed the place. Might as well. . . .

"What about a drink of the stuff you just poured for that gentleman?" he said, waving toward the end of the bar.

Stella threw his towel over his shoulder. "You think you need another one?" she asked.

Chipper pulled off his cap and laid it on the bar. "Stella, my girl, you can't serve me what I most need," he said. "So I think a drink will do just fine."

Stella's lips twitched as if she wanted to say something else, but she just grunted and pivoted to pick up a glass. A second later, she slapped the glass onto the bar and poured scotch into it. Chipper reached for his money but found nothing in his pockets. Confused, he checked his wallet. It was empty. He riffled his pockets again, pants, then jacket. No luck. He thought back to the last time he'd seen his money—not too long ago, right here in the bar. Had he left the money somehow? Lost it? He didn't know. A rush of panic hit him—how could he buy back the bicycle if he'd lost his money? He wanted to check the floor, fall down on his hands and knees to see if the money had fallen earlier, gotten wedged under the bar. But how could he do that? Admit to Stella that he'd drunk so much he'd lost his money? Giving into his pride and unable to think of anything else to do, he pointed to his glass.

"Better take that back," he said to Stella. "Seems I'm clean out of cash and didn't realize it."

Stella grunted. "You're good for it, no problem."

The man in the brown suit shifted and stood, and Chipper glanced his way. The man smiled and slid down to the stool next to his. Chipper noticed his shoes—brown wing tips without a scratch, no mud either.

"I'll cover that," said the man, indicating the drink.

"No need," said Chipper. "Stella knows I'll pick it up later."

"No, I insist." The man pulled out a stack of dollars.

"Suit yourself," said Chipper, seeing no need to argue further. "And thanks." Silence came to the room. Chipper sipped the scotch, wondered where his money was. The truck maybe, wedged in the seat. He decided to worry about it later.

"A beastly night," said the man. "You stranded?"

Chipper examined the stranger closer, noting again the unusual way he talked. The man's eyes were lively, sparkling with a curious light.

"Might say that," Chipper said. "Wife's over in Asheville. They shuttin' down the roads."

"So I hear."

"You?" Chipper faced the stranger.

"My name is Gabe," said the man, as if Chipper had asked. "I'm passing through here on the way South. The foul weather made travel impossible." He touched his glass to his lips but then sat it down again without drinking from it.

"I'm a long way from home," he said, twirling the glass in his fingers. "Much to my displeasure."

"Yeah, tell me about it," grumbled Chipper.

The man faced him. "You seem troubled," he said.

Chipper grunted and took a swallow of the liquor. It felt warm in his throat, but a cut of guilt hit him as it slipped down.

"Troubled is one word for it."

"A shame," said Gabe. "A man your age. About twenty-seven, I'd say. Same as me."

Chipper nodded. "Twenty-seven exactly."

"You a veteran?"

Chipper nodded again, started to take another drink, but then hesitated. "Pacific operations," he said. "Nineteen and forty three to nineteen and forty five. Quite a party."

"I did Europe," said Gabe. "England at first, then France toward the end." He twirled the drink but still didn't taste it.

"That happen over there?" Gabe indicated Chipper's stump.

"Didn't lose it milkin' cows, that's for sure." Chipper took another shot of booze to temper his sarcasm, but it tasted vile in his throat, a razor blade of heat cutting into his soul.

Silence came to the two men. Leaving the bottle of scotch on the bar, Stella walked to the back room.

"You married?" Chipper asked, hoping to make amends for his sharp remark.

"Was," said Gabe. "Until a year or so ago."

"What happened?"

Gabe held up his glass as if extending a diamond for inspection. "I imbibed too much of the grape," he said, smiling sadly. "Thankfully, we had no children."

"I got two," said Chipper. "A third on the way."

"But you know the problem of which I speak." It came out a statement, not a question.

Chipper's brow furrowed. How did Gabe know so much about him? He swiveled to study the man more closely. "You're a wise man," he said. "A regular genius."

Gabe lifted a shoulder in a shrug and sat his glass on the bar. "Years talking to bartenders will make a man a genius."

Chipper sipped the last of his scotch and put the glass down. Seconds passed. Chipper picked up the scotch bottle and poured another shot. He stared at the amber liquid. It seemed to mock him, its color a live thing daring him to leave it alone. Fighting the temptation, Chipper twisted away and stared into the fireplace. The flames licked up the chimney toward the cold outside. Bing Crosby started singing again, "I'll be home for Christmas." Chipper decided he hated the song. A strange sense of detachment overwhelmed him. Maybe it was the cozy surroundings. Or perhaps the bump on the head. But whatever it was, he suddenly felt weird, out-of-his-body, watching but not participating in the surroundings.

As if drawn by a magnet, he turned back and faced Gabe. The man's blue eyes seemed to grab him and pull him in. Gabe smiled, his teeth as white as the sleet outside. The smile made Chipper feel oddly secure, comfortable that he could tell Gabe anything and it'd be okay. The stranger in the new hat would listen to him without judgment, without condemnation.

"Tell me what to do, Mr. Genius," he said softly. "Tell me how to stop drinking, how to make things right with the wife who's just left me. Can you do that, Mr. Genius? Can you?"

His smile gone, Gabe took off his hat. A shock of wavy brown hair fell over his forehead. He twirled the hat on his right index finger. The twirling hypnotized Chipper.

"We're two peas in a pod," Gabe said calmly, watching the hat. "Same age, both of us veterans, both of us with a taste for the bottle, both alone on a Christmas Eve, no family near to love us. Both of us present, right here and right now, men without hope, without . . ." his voice trailed away.

Chipper started to protest the comparison. He did not want to admit his likeness to the man beside him—a man with no wife, no family. The likeness scared him worse than anything he'd ever faced, worse than guns pounding overhead, bayonets jammed toward his stomach, worse than anything but—

He pushed away the thought but knew he couldn't argue with Gabe's words. The stranger had nailed it right on the head.

As if talking to himself, Gabe continued now, his words like sandpaper scraping an open wound. "I can't tell you how to stop drinking any more than anyone could tell me. That's the way of our weakness. Only the one suffering from the affliction knows how to fight it, how to win over it. If you can't—

"But I can't beat it!" argued Chipper, breaking out of the hypnotic spell. "I've done everything I know to do." He picked up his glass. The liquor seemed to smile at him. He could taste it, smell it, feel it inside his stomach. He wanted it worse than anything he'd ever wanted, needed it like a man with asthma needing air. He slammed the glass down on the bar. Scotch spilled over the side. He had an unbearable urge to bend over and lick up the liquor before it ran to the floor.

"It's like a . . . like a trap that's caught me," he seethed. "And the teeth are too strong. They're cuttin' me up, bit by bit, and I can't . . . can't . . . ." His anger building, Chipper rose from the stool, his cap in his hand, his eyes on the spilled scotch as it spread out on the bar, the temptation swelling with each second.

"The anger that you feel right now," said Gabe, spinning his hat. "Use that in your fight. But direct it at the pain inside you, the pain you still need to face. You have that advantage over me. You can still face this beast. It can be beaten. Amends can be made for what you've done. You can be changed. You can start over. You can go to your wife, love her, and let her love you!"

Gabe continued to talk, but Chipper no longer heard. His heart pounding, he forced his eyes away from the scotch. Not knowing exactly what he planned but knowing he had to run before the booze sucked him in one more time, this time maybe forever, he shoved on his cap and stepped to Gabe.

"Hey, I . . . I need . . ."

"Go," said Gabe, his hat still spinning. "I understand." He stopped the hat and held out his hand. Chipper took it, gave it a quick shake, noticed a tattoo in the flesh between the thumb and index finger. He froze in place, staring at the tattoo. It looked like—

"The war," said Gabe, noticing his focus. "All sorts of men take hold of their little symbols during a war."

His mind reeling but feeling too scared and confused to ask any questions, Chipper nodded, pumped his hand once more, and rushed from the bar. At his truck, he stopped and bent over, his heart thumping, his breath short and ragged. The tattoo! But how in the world—? Suddenly realizing he had to know more about it, he twisted and ran back inside, his eyes searching for Gabe. Stella stood at the bar, her towel in its same resting place on her shoulder.

"Where is he?" asked Chipper. "Where's the man in the brown suit?"

Stella shrugged. "Gone," she said. "I came back from storage. Nobody here."

Head pounding, Chipper ran to the men's room but found no one. Though feeling foolish, he checked out the ladies' room, too. It was empty. Back in the bar, he studied Stella for several seconds.

"You got a back exit?" he asked.

Stella pointed to a door just past the fireplace.

Chipper ran to it, but it was locked, a metal bolt snugly in place, and no sign of anyone coming or going. Turning back, he didn't see Stella. He moved to the door of Stella's office.

"You sure you didn't see him?" he called.

Stella looked up from her desk and shook her head. "You look like you saw a ghost," she said.

Shrugging, Chipper pivoted and walked away. By the bar, he saw the bottle of scotch. Without thinking or knowing why, he grabbed the bottle and shoved it under his jacket. He'd pay Stella back, he told himself. Just as soon as he found the money he'd lost.

In the truck again, he shoved the bottle under the seat and rubbed Thumper behind the ears.

"He had a tattoo," he told Thumper. "A tattoo with the same emblem as the patch on Mose' cape."

Thumper licked Chipper's hand.

6

A DANGEROUS JOURNEY

*H*is thoughts bouncing around in his skull like the silver ball in a pinball machine, Chipper turned on the truck but didn't drive off just yet. He just sat there, tying to make some sense of what he'd just seen.

"It's crazy," he whispered to Thumper. "Plumb crazy." He thought of Mose and Gabe, the emblem on Mose' patch and Gabe's tattoo. What did it mean? Did it mean anything? Or was it just a coincidence?

Had to be coincidence, he decided. What else? Some weird convergence of the supernatural? A message that somebody—or something—wanted to pass on to him? But what message? And why send it to him?

"I'm losing it," he said, rubbing his eyes as if to wipe away what he'd seen. "Goin' plumb loco."

Chipper wondered for a second if he had imagined the similarity in the two emblems. Maybe he'd had enough scotch to cause hallucinations. But Mose did have a patch, and Gabe had a tattoo beside his thumb . . . and Chipper had never seen the symbol before.

Chipper rubbed Thumper's head and tried to convince himself he'd figured it out. Somehow, and for some reason he couldn't fathom, he had tied the two together, had melded the two images into one. But why? What connection did he see between Mose and Gabe?

Tired from thinking about it, he lay his head on the steering wheel and tried to get a grip on his emotions. The ache over his eyes appeared again, a pounding like a man with a shovel banging away behind the bridge of his nose. He thought of the bottle under the seat, how it could relieve the pain in his head. Just one shot, he told himself, one to stop the pain. He rejected the idea. But the craving kept coming, seeping into his throat, his stomach. Unable to fight it any longer, he grabbed the bottle and chugged down a quick gulp.

Wiping his mouth, he held the bottle for a second at his side. The drink's heat warmed him, soothed his loneliness. He lifted the bottle to take another shot, but stopped in mid-air. He thought of Mose and Gabe, what they had said, what they represented. He dropped the bottle and screwed the lid back tight. He looked at Thumper, the taste of guilt now strong in his mouth.

"I don't know, Thumper," he mumbled. "I just don't know."

Thumper licked his hand. His tongue was warm. Chipper knew instantly what he needed to do. "I need Reba," he said. "She'll know what all this means."

Thumper wagged his tail.

"We goin' to Asheville," said Chipper, momentarily

pushing away his questions about Mose and Gabe. "I don't care about the bad roads." He put the truck in gear and pulled onto the highway.

Thumper stared out the window as if checking for a stop sign.

"We goin' to find Reba," continued Chipper, shoving the bottle under the seat. "Bring her and my babies home." Driving carefully, Chipper kept his eyes on the road. The sleet and snow continued to fall, the mix of the two—one soft and one hard as small rocks—made the night seem confused, not quite sure what it wanted to become. Other than the weather and engine, a heavy silence fell over the truck, a silence so deep it seemed to Chipper that someone had wrapped a woolen scarf around the world. The quite even affected Thumper. He had his head on his front paws, his mouth closed in a grim frown.

Turning left, Chipper eased the truck onto the main road to Asheville, an asphalt highway leading the last few miles to the home of Dennis and Betsy Fuller. The asphalt gave the truck a little better traction than the gravel road out of Buckview, but Chipper didn't relax much. A layer of white at least two inches deep lay on the road. The lights of the truck danced off the white, creating an eerie glare from the road.

A sense of loneliness again rushed through Chipper, and his eyes watered. What if Reba refused to come home? She had plenty of reason to say no, to mistrust anything he said, any promises he made. Hadn't he made promises over and over again only to break them every time? He thought of the drink he had just taken, how he had no power to fight the pull of the bottle.

"I don't deserve her," he told Thumper. "Don't know why she ever married me in the first place." His memories drifted back to the first time he ever saw Reba. Her folks lived in Buckview then. She sat beside him in the first grade, her black curls tight on her head, her sky blue dress, white bobby socks, and shiny black shoes fit enough to wear to a queen's coronation. He loved her at first sight. But it took almost nine years for her to pay any attention to him. . . .

One day in the spring of his freshman year he rounded the corner of his high school and saw Reba and a boy named Jessie Watts. Two years older than Chipper and Reba, Watts had a reputation as a lady's favorite. He combed his black hair in a rakish wave and drove a brand new Ford with white-walled tires and a radio. His daddy was the mayor of Buckview.

Reba and Jessie stood under a tall maple tree, her back touching the tree trunk. Jessie had his right arm propped over her left shoulder, his palm on the tree bark. Jessie bent close as if to kiss her.

His heart falling to his shoes, Chipper ducked back behind the school. But then, unable to stop himself, he peered around to watch. He saw Reba duck away from the kiss. But Jessie moved quickly, a hand now on either side of her, pinning her back against the tree. Reba squirmed away, but Jessie persisted. He had a hand on her elbow now, pulling her closer.

Chipper heard Reba speak, her voice shaky. "No," she said. "Don't."

"Oh, come on," coaxed Jessie, still pulling at her. "You never been kissed like I can kiss."

"Leave me alone," squirmed Reba, trying again to escape.

"You want me to kiss you," insisted Jessie. "You know you do."

"You're hurting me," said Reba with a tinge of fear. "I'm not—

Chipper had seen enough. Charging across the schoolyard, he threw a shoulder into Jessie's back before the boy knew what hit him. Dragging Jessie away from Reba, Chipper jerked his arm around and twisted it toward his shoulder blade.

"She said 'no,' you big jerk. Or can't you hear?" He pulled the arm tighter.

Jessie twisted toward him. "Who do you think you are?" he screamed. "This is no concern of yours."

"I'm makin' it my concern!" hissed Chipper. "You ever bother her again and I'll . . . I'll break this arm and the other one too." He yanked Jessie's wrist once more, just to make sure the boy knew he meant business. "You got that?"

Though Jessie growled, he nodded his head "yes, he understood," and Chipper dropped his arm and stepped back. Cursing under his breath, Jessie rubbed his arm a second and then faced Chipper. "This ain't over Gaines," he said. "Not by a long shot."

"It's over for you and her," said Chipper, glancing at

Reba, who stood wide-eyed by the tree. "I don't care what happens to me. But you best not ever bother her again."

Sliding a comb through his hair, Jessie smiled, winked at Reba, and walked away. Chipper stepped toward her.

"Did he hurt you?" he asked.

"No, I'm okay." She glanced at the ground, then back at him. "Thanks," she said. "He . . . he scared me."

Still angry, Chipper ground his teeth. "Girl like you shouldn't ever be scared," he said. "I mean never."

Reba started walking, and he fell in step beside her. Fifteen minutes later they reached the front door of her white, two-story house. For the next three years they walked the same path almost every day, their early friendship gradually evolving into mutual love. He didn't kiss her until near the end of their junior year, and when he did, he felt that heaven had somehow placed itself on the edge of his lips . . .

Turning right, Chipper sighed heavily. A girl like Reba should "never be scared" he'd said on that day he first walked her home. But he had done more to scare her than any ten "Jessie Watts" could ever have done. He had scared her for over six years now, ever since he came home from the war. . . .

Chipper saw the city limits sign outside of Asheville. Ice covered it from top to bottom. "Almost there," he whispered, pressing harder on the gas. A minute later he reached the first red light of the business district on the main street. Christmas lights hung over the street, their colors bright and steady. The red light turned green as he approached it, and he zipped under it, his fingers tight on the wheel. Thumper stood up on the passenger seat, his ears pricked, his nose working the air. Chipper heard a pop. The truck pulled hard to the right, and Chipper fought the steering wheel. The right front tire felt mushy. Chipper hit the brakes but not too hard and the truck rolled to a stop. Chipper hopped out and ran around to the front right of the vehicle. Staring at the flat tire, he bit his tongue to keep from cursing. He bent over and saw a ragged gap in the rubber. Shaking his head, Chipper looked up and down the road but saw no one. No wonder. Only fools ventured out on a night like this. He took a deep breath. Okay. Nothing to do but hoof it.

Back in the truck, he turned off the engine, grabbed the right hand of a set of beat-up work gloves and a flashlight from under the seat, and patted Thumper. "Gotta walk a mile or so," he said, his mouth set. "But we can do it if we've a mind to, you know we can. Nothin' but a nice chilly walk to Reba and the kids. " Thumper barked.

Slipping on the glove, Chipper thought of the bottle of scotch. A drink would sure warm him up some, he figured. With a mile or so to walk and only a thin jack-et to protect him against the weather, who would blame a man for taking a swig or two along the way? He grabbed the bottle, shoved it under his jacket, and hopped out of the truck. His cap shoved as tight as possible over her ears, he leaned into the wind and headed toward downtown Asheville, with Thumper at his heels. Reba's folks lived just beyond the city limits on the other side, less than a mile past downtown.

Chipper quickly checked the sky. The sleet had slowed but not stopped. He felt the white pellets tapping onto his head and shoulders. He glanced down at Thumper, saw sleet bouncing off his back. "You okay?" he asked, touching the dog's head as he walked.

Chipper shivered. Remembering the scotch in his jacket, he pulled it out as he walked, opened it, and held it to his lips. He thought of Reba. What if she smelled it on his breath when he walked in? His hand shaking, he recapped the bottle, shoved it under his jacket, and kept walking. He heard his feet crunching the ice and snow. Other than that, no sound but the wind. He looked at his hand, saw the last two fingers poking through the ends of the glove. He thought of Mose, his long fingers hanging out of his gloves like black ice cycles. A new wave of guilt hit then, a mountain of self-remorse. Gritting his teeth, he pushed off the feeling and walked faster. "Just get to Reba," he thought. "Get to Reba."

7

A CLOSE ENCOUNTER

*T*he sidewalk lay covered in sleet and snow, and Chipper had difficulty keeping his balance as he walked up Main Street. Lifting his feet high, he led Thumper on a zig zag path, avoiding the areas where the ice had banked up the deepest. Though many of the storefronts displayed bright Christmas arrangements, he had his eyes on another focus and barely noticed. He lifted a foot and placed it down, lifted a foot and placed it down.

The frigid night air had frozen his nose and ears and was fast making headway into his feet. He had his hand stuffed into the pocket of his jeans and his stump wedged as tightly as possible against his side. His breath rolled out in thick white puffs, and his shoulders shuddered. He again remembered the bottle under his jacket but gritted his teeth and kept walking.

He lifted a foot, sat it down, lifted a foot, sat it down, lifted a foot. He heard a car approaching from behind and twisted toward it. His heel slipped, and he staggered against a telephone pole, his shoulder banging it.

He threw out his hand to stay upright. A splinter from the telephone pole jabbed into his index finger and he jerked away, a speckle of blood running down from the first knuckle. The bottle under his jacket fell out and crashed to the ground, spilling scotch all over his shoes. He saw the glare of a red light bounce off one of the storefront windows. A siren wailed for a short blast and then stopped. He rubbed his finger on his jeans, his eyes on the car now pulling to a stop by the curb, its red light still flashing. The door opened, and a policeman threw a beam of light into his eyes.

"Evenin'," called the policeman, walking toward Chipper. "You all right?"

Chipper nodded. "Yeah, don' fine."

The policeman stood five feet away now, his flashlight at his side, a quizzical furrow on his face.

"Kinda cold to be out on foot on Christmas Eve," he said. "That your truck back on the road?"

"Had a flat goin' to the in-laws—bad luck, huh?"

The policeman nodded. "They live close?"

Chipper pointed to the right. "A mile or so, not far."

"They got names?" His tone sounded suspicious.

"The Fullers," he said. "Dennis and Betsy. You know 'em?"

"I heard the names. They expectin' you?"

Chipper shrugged, unsure whether to lie or not. "My wife's there," he said. "We need to talk."

The policeman wrinkled his nose. "You had yourself some Christmas spirit?" he asked, his tone bordering on the unfriendly.

Chipper dropped his eyes. The smell of the scotch saturated the air. "A couple of drinks, nothin' more."

The policeman squatted, picked up the neck of the broken bottle. "How much of this you drink before drivin'?"

Chipper shuffled his feet. He thought of all the liquor he'd consumed at Stella's, and the drinks he'd taken from the bottle. "More 'en I needed," he admitted. "But I ain't hurt nobody by it, and my drinkin' didn't cause my flat tire."

The policeman stood, the neck of the bottle in his hand. "Maybe you ought to come on with me," he said. "Let's get some coffee in you, let me check with your in-laws. Then maybe I take you on over there, outta this weather. That sound all right?"

Chipper hesitated. If he went with the policeman, and the office checked with Reba before taking him to the Fullers, she might not understand. The policeman might even tell her he'd found a bottle of scotch at his feet. That'd make her madder than a cat taking a bath, and he didn't need that. She'd never talk to him if she thought he'd had more to drink. He licked his lips and tried to figure what to do. The policeman moved to him, touched him on the elbow.

"We won't take long," he said. "Down to the station, I'll leave you there with some coffee, go check on your folks, come back and take you over there."

Chipper gritted his teeth. If a police car pulled up in front of Reba's folks on Christmas Eve, they'd never let him hear the end of it. For the rest of his days, even if he and Reba did work things out, the Fullers would hold it against him. Think about the neighbors!

Jerking away, Chipper ducked behind the telephone pole and sprinted across the street, his feet moving faster than he could ever remember. From behind, he heard Thumper also running, his big feet padding across the ice. Rushing down Main Street, he reached the end of the block and turned right. Glancing over his shoulder, he saw the policeman hot after him, his flashlight beam pointing in his direction.

Concentrating straight ahead again, he came to the end of another block and turned left. He heard the sound of music and ran toward it. Twenty yards ahead, he saw a door open. A man and woman stepped entered a storefront through it, the man's arm around the woman's back. From behind, he heard the policeman yelling, but the cop hadn't turned the corner yet, and Chipper kept running. At the door where the man and woman had disappeared, he ducked inside the building, hoping the policeman hadn't seen him. Shutting the door, he patted Thumper and quickly scanned the room, searching left and right for the couple he'd seen. They were nowhere in sight. Catching his breath, he realized he had come into the building from which the music had escaped. Rubbing cold sweat off his forehead, he took a second to look around.

To his surprise, he realized that he'd walked head first into the front vestibule of a small, store-front church.

8

FROM THE MOUTHS OF BABES

*H*is head pounding with tension, Chipper quickly surveyed the area—no more than a sixteen by eighteen entry space with light brown walls, a picture of Jesus to the left, a small table with a white candle slightly off center to the right, and a rectangular brown rug that had seen more feet than a busy podiatrist in the center. He saw a set of plain white doors, dead ahead, one of them with the handwritten word "SANCTUARY" marked right in the middle. A second door, this one single and small, was off to the right, past the table and candle. The music sifted out from within the double doors—a congregation singing a throaty but ill-keyed rendition of "Joy to the World." The smell of peppermint and stale fish hung in the air. He remembered that the building once housed a seafood restaurant. To his relief the vestibule was empty.

His first impulse was to turn and flee, but he knew the policeman waited somewhere on the street to haul him off to jail. Turning back to the entry, he saw a single bolt on the door and twisted it so that it locked.

To his left, the small door suddenly opened, and he pressed up against the wall as if to hide. The front end of a wheelchair rolled out from behind the door. Chipper looked around the vestibule for a way out, but none presented itself. If he walked through the double doors, he'd step into the sanctuary, interrupting the service. But if he turned and ran into the street, he would no doubt renew acquaintances with the cop.

Resigned, Chipper watched as the wheel chair fully emerged. To his surprise, a small boy sat in it, his legs hanging down as the dead limbs of a fallen tree. A pair of clean blue jeans encased the spindly, inert limbs and black brogans, also new, hung off the small feet.

Raising his eyes, Chipper saw a blonde-headed, gray-eyed boy no more than ten years old. He had his hair slicked back and wore a red and black checkerboard flannel shirt, the top button buttoned. The boy smiled and showed a set of straight white teeth, the two in the top middle missing.

"My name's Michael" said the boy, his eyes bright with curiosity. His hands gripped the wheels of his chair, rolling it slightly forward then slightly back, a constant movement but without going anywhere. "What's yours?"

Though hesitant, Chipper didn't see a way to avoid the boy's question. "Folks call me Chipper," he said.

Michael held out a tiny hand, and Chipper took it. Michael's grip was firm, and his skin felt warm and smooth. For some strange reason, Chipper didn't want to let go of the hand, but the boy smiled again and pulled it away. "My friends call me Mikey," he said. "You got a nice dog." He pointed to Thumper, who waited patiently by Chipper's side.

"His name's Thumper," said Chipper. "He's a good boy."

"You here for church?" asked Mikey.

"Not exactly," Chipper said, not wanting to tell the boy a direct lie.

"What's that mean, 'not exactly'?"

"Well . . . uh . . . it means I just came in off the street," stammered Chipper. "It's warm in here, you know?"

"Don't you have a house?" Mickey rolled the chair forward, then back, forward, then back.

Chipper swallowed, surprised by the boy's directness. "Sure," he said. "I got a house."

"You smell funny," said Mikey, twitching his nose.

From behind, Chipper heard the entry door handle jiggle. The policeman! He glanced around the room, his eyes frantic.

"Somebody's at the door," whispered Mikey, the chair still for once. "You gone let 'em in?"

Chipper twisted to the door, then faced Mikey again. "There any other way out of here?" he asked.

"You runnin' from something," said Mikey, a statement of fact, not a question.

Chipper studied his shoes, unable to answer, not wanting to say anything untrue to such a sweet boy. The door jiggled again. "This is officer Stealy," called the policeman. "Please open the door."

His heart in his throat, Chipper moved toward the sanctuary. He'd duck into the church, he decided, and look for an exit from inside. Surely they had another door.

"Pssssst!"

He pivoted back toward Mikey, who was waving toward the small door by the candle. "In here," said Mikey. "Follow me!" Without another word, he rotated the wheelchair and rolled through. The entry door jiggling harder behind him, Chipper knew he had no choice. Leading Thumper, he felt the hair on the back of his neck stand to attention.

"Close the door!" ordered Mikey, his voice full of an unexpected authority. "You're safe in here."

Chipper obeyed without hesitation, and turned back around, his eyes now on the boy who sat so confidently in the wheelchair. The room was small, little more than a pantry, but a pair of sconces hung on the wall directly opposite where Chipper stood. A white candle burned in each of the sconces, the light casting a soft glow on Mikey's blonde hair. A high window covered with curtains was the only other break in the wall. But the window was air tight. Chipper felt suddenly hot in the small room, almost to the point of perspiring.

"It's safe here," said Mikey, backing his wheelchair to a spot just below the two sconces and pointing Chipper to a single wooden chair directly opposite him. "Nobody will bother us."

Taking the seat, Chipper had the weird sense that

Mikey was granting him an audience of some kind, a
young prince providing time for a subject to ask for a
favor. A question suddenly came to Chipper. "Where
are your folks?" he asked, trying to get a handle on the
situation. "Your ma and pa?"

"Got none," said Mikey, his tone nonchalant. "I
take care of myself." He rolled forward, then backward,
hands busy as always with the chair.

"You got no ma and pa?" asked Chipper, a deep sadness overwhelming him.

"We don't have long," said Mikey, obviously not
wanting to pursue the matter. "Officer Stealy won't
give up."

Though Chipper wanted to find out what happened
to Mikey's folks, he sensed that the boy was right. He
didn't have long.

"You know Stealy?" he asked.

"I know most folks in Asheville. Why's he after
you?"

His body heating up even more, Chipper wanted to
melt in the chair. How could he tell this boy about his
drinking? But he knew he couldn't lie to the child.
He'd done enough bad things for one night, he would-
n't add another to it. "He . . . he thinks I had too much
to drink."

"Did you?" Mikey stopped moving the chair.

Chipper stared at Mikey, but the boy didn't blink.
Who is this kid, Chipper wondered, amazed at the wisdom hiding in his youthful eyes. What made him so
sure of himself? And why did he feel so compelled to

tell him the truth? An urge to reveal everything ran through Chipper, a desperate desire to pour out everything bad that had ever happened to him, all of it . . . even the war. But how could he do that? Expose a child to all that horror? He moved back to safer ground.

"Yeah, well . . . who's to say what's too much to drink?" He slipped out of his jacket and lay it on his legs.

Mikey shook his head, obviously not satisfied with the answer. "What made Mr. Stealy think you'd been drinking?"

"He . . . he smelled it on me. I spilled it on my shoes."

"That what that smell is?" The chair rolled, retreated, rolled, retreated.

Chipper smiled. The boy didn't even know what liquor smelled like. Such an innocent child. He thought of Kyle Lee, how innocent he was . . . well . . . how innocent he had been. But lately he had disturbed some of his son's innocence, upset it with his own troubles—troubles he'd not had when he was Kyle Lee's age, Mikey's age. A yearning for his own early years ran through his bones, the years before his momma died.

"Yeah, it's scotch. A bottle broke, spilled all over me."

"It smells bad, I don't like it."

"Well, lots of people agree with you. But others . . . well, it has a way of makin' you want it . . . in a mighty powerful way."

Mikey stilled the chair. "I don't know about that,"

he said. "But drinking seems like such a waste."

Chipper shrugged but didn't feel near so indifferent as he hoped he appeared. Inside his head, he felt a need to justify himself, to explain the value of drinking. For some reason it seemed important that Mikey think well of him, almost as if he could make up to Kyle Lee for selling his bicycle if he could make Mikey understand.

"Drink relaxes a man," he started. "Makes it easy to handle some things."

"What happened to your arm?" asked Mikey, dismissing his efforts at explanation.

Chipper heard a muffled sound from behind the door and realized that someone was talking in the vestibule. Stealy?

"The war," he said, his ears pricked.

"That when you started drinking?"

He heard a loud squeak, then the voices moved away.

"They went into the sanctuary," said Mikey. "Those doors squeak awful bad."

Chipper took a deep breath and gave his attention to Mikey once more. "What happened to your legs?" he asked, hoping to deflect Mikey's question.

"Never had any," said Mikey. "The wheelchair is my legs."

Chipper grunted. "Life's no bargain, is it?"

Mikey tilted his head as if to question the premise of the statement. "You don't sound happy," he said.

Chipper grunted again. "You could say that. Why should I be? You either for that matter."

"Your lost arm make you sad?"

"Oh, that's not all of it," said Chipper, head down, eyes wanting to fill.

"I'm sorry," said Mikey. "Sorry you feel sad tonight."

"I've got a boy about your age," said Chipper. "And a wife and daughter, too. I . . . I want to get home to them."

"I'm ten," said Mikey. "They want to see you."

"I'm not so sure," said Chipper, mumbling to himself as much as to Mikey. "I'm not a good man."

Mikey rolled over and lay a hand on his arm. "Everybody does wrong sometimes," he said. "Just don't keep on doing wrong."

For several long seconds, Chipper studied the worn carpet on the floor. When he looked up, he saw Mikey staring at him, the compelling eyes drilling into his heart. "Aren't you sad about your legs?" Chipper asked.

"No," said Mikey, his chair still. "Not really. I mean, hey, I got all I need. A warm bed, food to eat. I see the sun come up every morning, stars twinkling. I can feel snow falling on my face. And I love puppies— cats too when they don't scratch."

Chipper shook his head, amazed at the boy. So wise for his age, but still so clear-eyed and naive, too. The boy was too good to be true. No legs and no parents, yet still as innocent as a fawn in the forest. So much like he used to be, back before his mama died trying to give birth to a brother for him, a brother that died when his mama did.

In some ways, his daddy had died that same Christmas eve, seventeen years ago. Though his daddy had pressed on the best he could, all the cheer went out of the house that night, the cheer that made life full and vibrant, the cheer that found joy in the sound of a waterfall and the touch of a baby's cheek.

As if struck by lightning, Chipper suddenly realized that though he had blamed much of his drinking on the war, the issue really went deeper than that, further back in his life. The loss of his mom when he was ten had started him on the path toward his problems, and the war had simply finished the job. He'd been so innocent back then, just like Mikey was now, so clear-eyed and hopeful. Mikey was just like him. Same hair and eyes, same age, same innocence. It was almost as if his past had come to life again, a reminder of what had been, what could never come again. His mood faltered as he thought of those days.

He heard the doors squeak again and the sound of voices. Standing, Chipper lay his jacket on the table and eased over to the door. He pressed his ear against it and listened for a long minute, but he couldn't tell if it was Stealy talking or not. He faced Mikey again.

"I need to get out of here," he said. "Don't want to spend Christmas Eve in jail."

Mikey nodded. "You need your family," he said. "And they need you."

"I hope they'll take me back."

"They will," said Mikey. "I know . . . believe me. A boy always wants his daddy. If you love them enough to change the wrong you've been doing, they will want you back."

Chipper bit his lip. Could he change that much? Could he go back and rediscover some of the innocence he'd lost? Become like Mikey, able to find good even in the midst of pain and suffering?

"The window," Mikey said, tilting his head toward the small square. "Go out the window. It opens to the alley."

Chipper stepped to the drapes and pulled them back. Pushing hard with his one hand, he managed to pop the window open. A swath of frigid air rushed over his head, and he turned back for his jacket. Mikey handed it to him. He slipped into it and shoved his cap down tight.

"I gotta go," he said, feeling sad about leaving Mikey. "Maybe I'll see you again soon."

Mikey shrugged. "Who knows?"

Though he knew Stealy was close by, Chipper still didn't want to leave. He felt like he needed to say something more, something better, more intimate.

"Look, I—

Mikey held up a hand. "Don't worry about it," he said. "Go to your family."

Chipper touched the boy's shoulder. "You're a good kid," he said. "Smart, too."

Mikey smiled. "Thank you," he said. "And merry Christmas."

Chipper sighed. "Merry Christmas to you, too." He stepped to the window, grabbed Thumper by the bottom and hauled him up and through it, dropping him head first to the street. Following quickly, he slipped feet first into the night air. Bouncing into the alley, he shoved his hand into his pocket and his stump into his side. He felt something in the left pocket. Hurriedly searching the pocket, he pulled out a brown paper sack. Momentarily forgetting about Stealy, he moved to a streetlight and opened it. His mouth dropped open and he ran back to the window and pulled up to look back into the room. But as he expected, Mikey was gone.

For a second he considered rushing back into the church and searching every nook and cranny of the place until he found him. But somehow he suspected the search would prove futile.

Dropping back to the ground, he led Thumper into a jog up the alley toward Main Street. In his hand he held a leather cord necklace he'd found in the paper sack. At the end hung a wooden object in the exact same shape as the patch on Mose' cape and the tattoo on Gabe's hand.

9

OPEN DOORS

*R*unning faster than he thought he could, Chipper pushed away his confusion about the leather necklace and covered the distance to the Fuller's house in less than twenty minutes. To his great relief, he found the lights still on even though he knew it had to be close to ten o'clock. Shivering, he rushed onto the wrap-around porch and knocked rapidly on the door. Waiting, he tried to come up with the right words for Reba, something to convince her to let him enter the house. The door opened. Mr. Fuller, a square man with a face like a block of wood, stood silhouetted against the lights of the house.

"Chipper?" he asked, surprise on his face.

"Uh . . . yeah, Mr. Fuller," he said, eyes down. "I'm here . . . here to see Reba." He raised his head. Mrs. Fuller, an older version of Reba, stepped up behind her husband. Mr. Fuller turned to her. "Chipper's here to see Reba," he said, as if announcing the time of day. Mrs. Fuller edged past him and took Chipper by the hand.

"Come in and close the door," she said. "You will get sick if you aren't careful."

Chipper accepted warily, wondering where Reba was. Inside, Mrs. Fuller steered him and Thumper to a fireplace in the den, handing him an afghan as he passed the sofa. Warming his freezing body by the fire, he wondered again about Reba and the children. Mrs. Fuller left the room, returned a moment later, and handed him a cup of coffee. Mr. Fuller took a seat in a recliner but didn't lean back.

"You said you're here for Reba?" Mrs. Fuller asked.

Chipper nodded and sipped the coffee. "It's . . . well . . . it's hard for me to say," he started. "But we . . . we had a fight. I came home . . . she wasn't there . . . figured she called you. I came . . . came to talk to her. Hope that's all right."

Mr. Fuller rubbed his chin. "You have been drinking," he said, his tone slightly accusatory. "That cause the fight with Reba?"

Chipper stared at his shoes, nodded his head.

"I don't blame Reba for leaving you," said Mr. Fuller. "She doesn't want you around the kids with that stuff."

Chipper started to defend himself but then had no heart for it. Mr. Fuller was right. "I . . . I just want to see Reba," he said.

"Fine by us," said Fuller. "But there's just this one thing."

Chipper steeled himself. Here it came. Reba had no doubt put the kids to bed, then joined them, leaving behind instructions that she didn't want to see him. He stared into his coffee.

"Reba isn't here," said Mrs. Fuller.

"She—?"

"She never came here," said Mr. Fuller. "Haven't heard from her since she called earlier this morning."

"But she has to be here!" argued Chipper, his mind racing. "Where else could she go?"

"Don't know," said Mrs. Fuller. "But we got no reason to lie. You can check the house if you want."

Chipper started to protest again but then knew that made no sense. He could see that the Fullers were telling the truth. But if Reba wasn't here, where was she?

"Is your phone working?" he asked.

Mr. Fuller shook his head. "Out the last few hours," he said.

Chipper stared into the coffee again. "I got to get home," he said. "Make sure Reba and the children are okay."

"I'm sure they're fine," said Mrs. Fuller, kinder than he remembered her being. "Maybe they went to a neighbor's house for a while. You just missed them when you came home."

Chipper nodded, appreciating her effort to make him feel better. But that didn't change his determination to go home.

"I didn't see your truck," said Mr. Fuller, a touch of challenge in his voice.

"Tire went flat," said Chipper. "On the road a mile or so back."

"Too dangerous to travel tonight," said Mr. Fuller.

"I'll take you in the morning."

Chipper turned and placed his coffee cup on the oak mantle over the fireplace. "I'm not waitin' until morning," he said, facing the Fullers again. "Not goin' have my kids wake up on Christmas without their daddy there."

"You should've thought of that before you—

Mrs. Fuller threw a sharp glance at her husband, cutting off his harsh words. Chipper hung his head. Mr. Fuller had it right, he decided. He should have thought of a whole lot of things before he gave into his drinking again. But he hadn't done what he should have done. He knew it, Reba knew it and the Fullers knew it. But that didn't mean he would stay put now and let things go from bad to worse.

"I'm goin' home," he said. "One way or the other. I can walk, you can loan me your car, or you can take me. It makes no difference. But I'm goin' just the same." He picked up his coffee, drank deeply again from it. "I thank you for the coffee," he said. "And the warmth of your fire." He handed the cup to Mrs. Fuller, who sighed and faced her husband. Mr. Fuller rubbed his forehead, his head in his hands.

"You sober enough to drive?" he asked.

"I'm plenty sober," said Chipper, thinking of Mikey from the church. "More sober than I've been in a long time."

"The roads are awful," Fuller said. "You really should wait until morning."

Thinking of the necklace Mikey had given him,

Chipper shook his head. No way he could wait all night to find out what all this meant. "I'm goin' tonight, " he insisted. "One way or the other."

Fuller gave up. "Take my car," he said. "It's got more gas than the truck." He reached into his pants' pockets and pulled out a set of keys. Looking up, Chipper faced the Fullers, his mind still on the necklace hanging around his neck.

"Listen," he said. "I know . . . know . . . I've messed up a bunch . . . well . . . more than a few times since . . . since I come into this family. But . . . I . . . I . . ." he wanted to say he planned to change all that, planned to turn over a new leaf, make himself into a different man. But he didn't feel strong enough to do that yet; he was not able to make that kind of promise without seeing Reba, without asking her what the necklace meant. Somehow he believed she'd know the secret to the strange encounters he'd had since he left home; she'd know how to interpret it all. And though he didn't want to think about it, he believed that the object held the key to whether or not she'd take him back after this, if she'd give him another chance to prove he could change.

"I need to go," he said. "And thank you for the use of your car."

Mr. Fuller nodded, his mouth grim.

Chipper led Thumper to the door. He faced the Fullers again. "I'm . . . I'm . . ."

"Find my daughter," said Mr. Fuller. "And do what you got to do to make things right by her. Then bring home my car."

"Go on," said Mrs. Fuller. "Call us in the morning."

Chipper left the house and climbed into Mr. Fuller's car, a black Chevrolet. Switching on the engine, he flipped on the heater, patted Thumper and backed out of the driveway. On the road, he thought again of the necklace he wore. Though he didn't know what he'd find when he reached home, he knew that one way or the other he'd never be the same after tonight. He'd find out what the necklace meant, and Reba would take him back, and he'd turn his life around; or the object would remain a mystery, and Reba would turn him away, and the liquor would take over his life for good. That would mean he'd leave Buckview and never see Reba and the children again. Touching the necklace with his stump, a shudder ran through Chipper's body.

Without Reba and the children, he had no motivation to change a thing. But with them . . . well . . . with them he'd find enough strength to change everything, no matter how hard.

10

LOST THINGS

*T*hough steering carefully, Chipper drove fast through the black night. His nerves jumpy, he kept seeing visions of Mose, Gabe, and Mikey—their faces a trio of question marks hanging in the air just past the windshield. Increasingly confused, he almost expected to see a fourth apparition pop up at any moment.

He tried to focus on what to say when he saw Reba. Tell her about the encounters with Mose, Gabe, and Mikey first? Ask her what she thought they meant? Or should he begin right out with the fact that he'd lost his job? That his latest round of drinking started when that happened? And what about the fact that he'd pawned Kyle Lee's bicycle? How could he ever admit to that?

The road slipped by. The sleet had stopped again, and he made better time than he had expected. Thumper lay quietly beside him, his eyes closed, apparently tired from the evening's adventures. Chipper sighed, his mood dropping again. At the church with Mikey, everything had seemed better, manageable even. But now? Bleak again as he faced the reality of having to tell Reba that he had lost the bike. He wondered again about Reba and the children. Where had they gone? Were they back home? Or had she taken the kids and left for good?

Trying to stay positive, he focused on the necklace and tried to figure out its message. Though he couldn't figure how or why or where from, the connection between the three encounters had to be more than mere chance. The same image showing up on three different people in one night made absolutely no sense. Yet it had happened. Like a dominant color running through a quilt, he knew there was a theme somehow—Mose, Gabe, and Mikey had brought a message to him, one that he had to decode if he had any chance to remake his life.

Steering momentarily with his knees, he pulled the necklace off and dropped it onto the seat. Glancing down, he tried to figure it out. What was it? What did it mean? No answer came to him, and he focused on the road again. Five more miles to Buckview. He glanced to Thumper.

"She at home, boy?" he asked hopefully. "Reba back home with Kyle Lee and Andrea Grace?"

Thumper opened his eyes but didn't answer.

"What am I gonna say to her?" he asked. "How can I tell her about that bicycle?"

Again no answer from Thumper. The miles slipped by. Chipper saw the sign to Buckview—only a mile and a half to go. His heart fell lower. Of all the things he'd ever done, selling the bicycle was the worst. Now he had to tell Reba. His eyes filled, and he found it tough to see the road. How could he face Reba and Kyle Lee without that bicycle? He couldn't do it, he decided, no matter what lousy excuse he offered. He had to find a way out of this mess, a way to undo what he had done. But how?

Wiping his eyes with his stump, he suddenly knew what he had to do. No matter how risky, he had to recover the bicycle. But he had no money, and Billy's had to be closed. He pressed the gas harder. A half mile later, he turned left and drove down Watson Street. Three blocks later, he turned left again, then right. The car slid to a stop in a dark alley behind the back door of Billy's Pawn Shop. The ice and sleet had knocked off the power. The sign with the missing letters wasn't blinking. His heart pounding, Chipper turned to Thumper.

"Not happy 'bout this," he said trying to convince himself.

Thumper whined but didn't argue.

"I can't go home without that bike," he said. "And I'll pay Billy back for it. He'll understand."

Thumper whined again, his tail sagging and his eyes darting out and back with uneasiness.

"I gotta do this," said Chipper, anxious for Thumper to understand. "Do a bad thing to make up for a bad thing."

Thumper lay his head on his paws. Chipper patted him on the head.

"You stay here boy," he said. "I'll come right back."

Thumper stayed still.

His cap tight on his head, Chipper told himself once more that he had no choice. He hopped out of the car, grabbed a lug wrench and flashlight from the trunk, and skulked to the back door. He hooked the edge of the wrench under the latch and pulled back hard. The wood cracked but didn't break. He jammed the wrench further under the wood and pulled once more, his whole body leveraged against the simple lock. The bolt caved this time and snapped off. The door sagged open, and Chipper rushed through it into Billy's shop. Stopping only long enough to close the door and turn on the flashlight, he eased across the concrete floor to the place where he'd last seen Billy with the bicycle. It wasn't there.

Surprised but not yet concerned, Chipper searched the room with his eyes. But still no bike. Moving slowly, he edged toward the corners of the storeroom. No luck. He stopped and took a breath. Where had Billy put the bike? Had he moved it to the front room where he kept the "for sale" items? But Billy had made him a promise! Had he forgotten what he'd said only a few hours ago?

His anxiety rising, Chipper left the storeroom and moved to the front of the shop, his hand touching the wall to keep from bumping into something in the cluttered building. The front room had more light from outside but still not enough to see clearly. Chipper eased his way to the front window display and saw several baby dolls, a small bassinet, at least three lamps, a rocking chair, two picture frames, and a scattering of other items. But no bicycle.

Turning, he checked over the rest of the room. All kinds of items—cabinets with glass fronts full of watches, sets of cheap china, picture frames, other bits and pieces of furniture, hubcaps and more hubcaps—sat silently in their places. But still no bicycle.

Shivering in the cold room, Chipper stopped again and considered the possibilities. Did Billy keep some things elsewhere? His home maybe? Chipper's hopes soared. Billy had taken the bike home so no one could see it! He had it there for him to pick up on Monday! How kind! But then he remembered Billy's house, a one-story brick that he shared with his wife and in-laws, a place too small for storage.

His spirits sagged as another possibility entered his head. Maybe Billy had sold the bike. Someone had come in right as he closed, a mom or a dad desperate for a gift for a child. The person had seen the bicycle and offered Billy a price he couldn't turn down. Was that possible? Would Billy stoop so low?

Chipper hung his head. He'd stooped low enough to pawn the bicycle. What made him think Billy wouldn't do something not half as bad?

Almost desperate now, he moved through the shop once more, his eyes raking every shelf, every counter-top, every hook on the wall, every corner, behind every door. But the bike wasn't there. Billy had sold it, no doubt about it. And Chipper was to blame.

A jolt of anger hit him. Not at Billy but at himself, a hot blaze of fury from deep in his soul. Now he'd never see the bicycle again, never get to give it to Kyle Lee. And it was his fault, nobody's but his!

His eyes filling, Chipper stepped to the cash register and jerked it off the counter. He held it over his head, his anger fueling the power in his right hand as he held it there for a second and wondered what to do. A scream rose in his throat as he rushed to the front window.

At the window he paused, hoisting the register even higher, his stump on one side to balance it, his right hand gripping it tightly. Opening his mouth to release the scream, he tensed his back and started to throw the register through the window. But then he saw—Mikey's face reflected in the glass. He stopped in mid toss, the scream dying in his throat. Lowering the register back against his chest, he studied the window again, but Mikey's face had disappeared as quickly as it had come.

A sense of utter defeat washed over him and he knew that any hope he'd had to reconcile with Reba had just died. Not only had he pawned the bicycle, but now Billy had sold it and he could never recover it. Reba might forgive him once more for his drinking, but she'd never forgive him for losing the one thing Kyle Lee wanted so much. To fail her was one thing. To betray one of her children was another. No matter what happened next, Chipper sensed deep in his bones that he'd burned his last bridge with his family.

Worn out from tension and grief, Chipper pivoted, placed the register back on the counter and slumped to the back door. In the car, he hugged Thumper tight.

"We'll go home one last time," he said, heartbroken.

Thumper licked his face, and Chipper sat still for several long minutes and let the tears run down his cheeks and onto the tongue of the only creature on earth that he believed still loved him.

11

HOME AGAIN

*I*t took Chipper less than fifteen minutes to drive the rest of the way home. But they were the longest minutes of his life. Every millisecond that ticked away felt like an eternity, a torturous stretch of time. His last hope gone, his body craved the numbing effects of a bottle—a bitter anesthesia to block out the incredible guilt that had overcome him. Though the hour had drawn past eleven thirty and Stella's had closed, he knew of a bootlegger who serviced clients like him for a premium price on a seven-days-a-week, twenty-four-hours-a-day basis. His foot hit the brakes, and he almost turned around to drive to the man's trailer. But then he touched the necklace lying on the seat and managed to fight off the temptation.

Finally, he made it home. But he didn't go inside immediately. Instead, he turned off the car and sat for several minutes, his heart thumping wildly. The house was still dark. He couldn't tell if Reba and the kids were home or not. He turned to Thumper.

"Whatcha think, boy?" he asked. "They already asleep?"
Thumper wagged his tail hopefully.

"I gotta know," Chipper whispered. "One way or
the other, I gotta know if Reba's gone."

Thumper whined. Chipper started to open the
door. He saw the necklace lying on the seat. He felt the
craving rise from deep within, desperate for a drink.
He picked up the necklace and slipped it over his head.
Tucking it under his shirt, he opened the door and
hopped out, Thumper behind him. Seconds later, he
eased through the front door of the house. The smell of
the Christmas tree hit him as he entered, but the room
was cold. He stepped to the wood stove and held his
hand over the top—cold, too. He swallowed hard,
stood dead still in the dark room, and tried to work
up enough courage to go into his bedroom. Thumper
stood at his knees, his nose poised in the air.

"I gotta see," Chipper said, moving to the bedroom.
"Gotta see." He opened the door and peered inside.
She wasn't there. He staggered back, his knees sagging,
his back sliding down the wall until he sat on the floor.
He threw his hand over his face and sobbed openly.

Thumper sat down beside him and poked his head
into his lap, but Chipper pushed him away. Rolls of
grief shuddered through him, and he wailed into the
dark night, his last hope crushed. Thumper poked at
him again. Chipper raised his eyes and stared at his dog
but didn't really see him. Inside his head, he saw Mose
again, the homeless apparition who had come from
nowhere to tell him of his future, a future with no wife

and no children, a future that now had come true. After Mose he saw Gabe, the image of his present, a present alone and in the dark with no where to go and no one to love him. And then came Mikey, the boy of his past, a boy still innocent and hopeful, a boy who knew suffering but hadn't let it make him bitter, a boy who smiled in the face of pain and so overcame it.

Each of the three had told him to change and had given him hope that he might do so. But now their encouragements had come up against the real world, a world where sometimes the chance for change passes before a person can act on it, the opportunity a fleeting thing, a door opening and closing, a sliver of time that comes but then disappears forever.

From deep inside, Chipper's grief turned to anger. He had wanted to change, he told himself, had come home to tell Reba of his newfound commitment to stop drinking. But she'd left him before he could and the fickle nature of his opportunity made him furious. Jerking up from the wall, he pulled the necklace over his head and stared at it for several long seconds, still trying to figure it out. But when no answer came to him, he became more and more angry.

He ran to the front room, opened the door, and stepped onto the porch clutching the leather cord. It seemed to burn into his flesh, a piece of mystery in his palm, a mystery that had promised so much but delivered so little.

Gritting his teeth, he held the necklace up once more, but still no clue came. He threw the object into the night. The necklace arched up and out of sight, and then it clicked as it hit the icy snow beneath the stand of oaks and pines by his house.

Moving without thought, he ran to his bedroom once more, pulled out a handful of clothes, and stuffed them into a paper sack. "They'll do better without me," he thought. "Better without a dad who can't beat the bottle, can't hold a job."

Carrying the sack to his closet, he hauled out the only two sweaters he owned, a belt, and four shirts. Loaded with most of his meager possessions, he rushed back out the front door. At the car, he started to step inside but Thumper ran to his side and barked. Chipper kneed him away.

"Stay here!" he commanded. "Stay with Kyle Lee!" Thumper barked again but Chipper didn't relent. He climbed into the car and turned on the engine. Thumper stood by the door and continued to bark, his body at attention. Chipper rolled down the window and stuck out his head. He heard something on the highway—a truck coming. Chipper started to move the car, but then he saw a light cutting through the trees that edged the road. The light turned his way and flickered down the street toward his house.

Confused, he sat still, his breath halted. The truck moved toward him, a big black thing with an engine loud enough to wake the dead. Chipper knew the vehicle—he'd driven it more than once.

Ty Bo? But what—?

The truck stopped in front of his house. The door

on the passenger side opened and a person jumped down and began to run his way. A lump the size of a boiled egg climbed into Chipper's throat. He switched off the engine, pushed open the door, and ran toward Reba as she rushed to him. The two of them came together in the middle of the yard, his arms around her neck, her cheek on his shoulder, tears on both their faces. For several seconds, they just stood there, neither of them speaking, each caught up in a moment that didn't need words, a moment made better by the silence they allowed.

A thousand thoughts crowded around in Chipper's head. Where had Reba been? Why had Ty Bo brought her home? Was she going to forgive him? Let him come home again?

He heard a truck door slam again and then saw Kyle Lee running across the yard. Ty Bo followed, a bundle of blankets and sleeping Andrea Grace in his arms. Stepping away from Reba, Chipper opened his arms and Kyle Lee joined the family embrace. Ty Bo handed the bundle to him, and Chipper stared down into the closed eyes of his daughter, his tears dripping onto the blankets. He faced Reba again, and she hugged him. Kyle Lee had him by the legs and Thumper stood beside all of them, wagging his tail.

"You're home," he whispered. "I thought—

"Inside," said Reba. "Let's get the kids out of the cold. I'll explain inside."

Too happy to argue, Chipper led everyone into the house, leaving Reba only long enough to throw some wood into the stove. Then he joined her and the rest of the group in the kitchen, where Ty Bo had coffee going. Joining Reba and Kyle Lee at the table, he took off his cap and hung it on the back of a chair. Taking Reba by the hand, he dropped his eyes and took a heavy breath.

"I got a story to tell," he said.

"So do I," said Reba.

"Maybe we ought to leave you two alone," said Ty Bo, turning from the coffee and nodding to Kyle Lee. "Give ya a few minutes to talk a bit."

Kyle Lee nodded, and Ty Bo led him out.

Chipper faced Reba, his heart in his throat. Now he'd find out what had happened, whether she would give him another chance.

"Before we start," he said. "I want you to know I love you."

Reba nodded. "I love you, too, Chipper. But we do need to talk."

"I know," he said. "Believe me, I know."

12

STORIES

*I*t scared me to death when I saw you had left," said Reba. "I knew you were upset about something, that you wouldn't have started drinking if you weren't. But I was so mad at you, I didn't give you a chance to explain. When I came back from the kids' room and saw you were gone, I sat right down and started crying. I realized that you needed me, but I acted spitefully toward you, harshly. I wanted you back, wanted to know what had happened. Then I remembered you had mentioned Ty Bo. You tried to tell me something, but I didn't listen."

"I've made too many excuses, too—

She held up a hand, cutting him off. "Let me get this said. All at once will be better."

He closed his mouth.

"I left Kyle Lee watching Andrea Grace," Reba continued. "Ran up to the Wilson's. Their phone was still working, thank the Lord. I called Ty Bo, asked him what happened. He told me about the job." She paused, her head down. "I'm sorry I didn't listen to you," she said. "But I was too impatient, too—well, anyway."

She stood and walked to the sink, took a drink, and faced him again. "Anyway . . . Ty Bo told me he had laid you off. I told him you had left, had been drinking. He offered to come over, to help me see if I could find you."

Chipper nodded. That explained where Reba had gone. She took another sip of water. "We left the kids with his wife," she said. "Then drove all over the place—the hardware, the grocery, the gas station. Ty Bo checked Stella's. She said you'd been there but left."

"I came back later," mumbled Chipper. "She told me Ty Bo had come in. But she didn't say you were with him."

"He didn't tell her that," said Reba. "No need for her to know we were having our troubles." She sat back down at the table, her hands wrapped around her water glass.

"Ty Bo and I didn't know where else to go. I asked him to take me to the church. If I couldn't find you, I wanted to pray for you." She dropped her eyes. "Billy Baldwin came in," she said. "He found me at the altar. He was there to set things up for the Christmas Eve service."

Chipper dropped his eyes too, his shame returning. "He tell you what I did?" he asked.

"Not at first. But he saw that I'd been crying and asked if I was okay. I didn't want to tell him anything, but I . . . I don't know . . . he's such an easy man to talk to, he listens so well . . . I needed somebody."

"It's okay," said Chipper. "You didn't do no wrong by telling him."

"He told me about the bicycle," said Reba, her tone even, her eyes on her water glass.

Chipper's eyes filled once more. "I'm sorry," he whispered. "It's low, I know it, and I hate myself for doin' it. I planned to buy it back—

"We'll deal with that later," said Reba. "Just let me finish."

He hung his head, and she continued. "While I was at the church, Ty Bo checked by Stella's again to see if you'd come back there. She said you had, but had left again. Also told him you had left some money there. She found it on the floor by the bar. Ty Bo came to the church to tell me."

Chipper's eyes widened. Stella found his money! Maybe he could buy another bike! But not before Christmas morning. Sad again, he refocused on Reba. "But you still didn't know where I was," he said. "I drove to your folks."

"I know," she said. "I'd tried to call them a few times before from the church, but the phone had been dead. When I finally got through, I asked them to pray for you too. They told me you had come. Told me you were headed back here. That's when I asked Ty Bo to bring me back home." She drank from her water.

"Ty Bo's done right by you," said Chipper. "He's a friend."

"You have lots of friends," said Reba. "More than

you think."

Chipper shrugged. "I hardly know Billy and Stella," he said. "Though I've lived here with them my whole life."

"They know you," said Reba. "Know you're a good man deep down. Know the war did something to you, something you're still trying to beat."

Chipper walked to the sink and ran a glass of water. "The war seems like a long way off," he said. "A long time ago."

"But it changed you," said Reba. "You've told me it did. But you never told me why."

Chipper glanced at his stump. "Some things hurt too much to tell," he said.

"Maybe the telling is the only way to end the hurt," said Reba. "Maybe it's the keeping that makes the pain so deep, so hard to fight. It's all caged up in you, like a mountain cat scratching from in to out, trying to escape. Maybe you let that cat go, it won't scratch you so much anymore."

Chipper sipped his water, his mind busy. Was this the time? The place? The opportunity to finally tell someone what had happened to him in the jungles of the Pacific? He face Reba, exhaled slowly. Maybe she was right. To deal with the hurt, he had to voice it. Now or never.

"We'd been pinned down almost twenty hours," he said quietly. "Japanese shelling us since the morning, and it was almost three a.m. At just past three, the ground assault started, more of the enemy than we'd ever seen. They came at us in the dark. My group, about thirty men, got cut off from the main body of the boys. We fought for over two hours, then the ammunition ran low. The hand to had started then, knives and bayonets, the butts of our rifles. One man against another, so close you could see the eyes of the people you killed, those who wanted to kill you. I heard my friends dyin' around me, one after another, cries of pain, prayers to God, the names of wives, children too."

He paused and sipped from his water, and then started again, his face blank. "I found myself alone, the last one left alive so far as I knew. I had blood all over me, stickin' to my face, my hair. Someone smacked me on the head and I fell, started to crawl away. I crawled and crawled . . . I don't know how far. The underbrush cut my arms, my legs and face. I thought I had escaped. Then the ground seemed to explode in front of me. But it wasn't a bomb. It was a trap, a buried metal trap of some kind . . . . I don't know. But it bit down into my left arm, snapped it below the elbow. I bit my tongue to stay quiet. It was almost daylight. I knew if I stayed there the enemy would find me. And all of us knew they didn't take prisoners, not at that stage of the war." He sipped his water. Reba stood and walked to him, but he waved her away.

"I knew I had to get free of that trap," he said. "But it was hooked to the base of a tree, the metal still good, sharp and strong, and I couldn't open it with one hand." His voice fell to a whisper and his eyes filled.

"No way to break it off the tree," he said. "Only one thing to do." Tears ran hard down his face.

"I had a knife," he said. "A knife for killin'. I used the knife to . . ." The tears flooded his cheeks and dripped onto the floor. 'To cut my way free," he said. "My own knife in my own flesh. My arm left behind . . . behind on the floor of the jungle . . . in that . . . that trap."

His head fell to his chest, and Reba ran to him and hugged him close. The two of them stood in the kitchen together, both of them covered with tears, both of their hearts broken by the evil of war, but both also rejoicing that Chipper Gaines had finally brought his story into the presence of someone who loved him enough to help him carry the burden.

13

CHRISTMAS MIRACLES

*P*ure snow replaced the sleet at just past two a.m., and by the time Chipper and Reba climbed out of bed at seven, the clouds had dropped at least five inches of soft, white powder on the ground. Quickly loading the stove with wood, Chipper joined Reba in the kitchen. She handed him a cup of coffee and pointed him to the table.

"You sleep any?" he asked.

"Not much. You?"

"Maybe an hour or so early this mornin'. A lot on my mind."

"Tell me about it."

He walked to her by the sink. She had her hands in flour, already making biscuits.

"What time you think we ought to wake the kids?" he asked, his tone almost scared.

"Soon as I finish these biscuits," she said. "If we don't wake them up then, they might beat us to it."

He sipped his coffee again, remembering the rest of

last evening. After thanking Ty Bo over and over again, they saw him off and put Kyle Lee to bed to join his little sister. Back in the kitchen, Chipper had told Reba his story, from the time he left home until the time he came back. He left nothing out, not even the part about running from the policeman in Asheville.

Reba had listened silently as he told the tale, her eyes wide in spots, her thoughts obviously confused. When he finished, she wrinkled her brow and asked him to describe the necklace one more time. But even after he did, she still didn't know what it was.

"I'll try to find it in the morning," he said. "It's out there in the yard somewhere."

"Maybe when the snow thaws," she said.

They'd gone to bed then, each of them aware that Chipper's battle with the bottle wasn't over but somehow sensing that at least they now had a fighting chance against it. They'd snuggled close as the night passed, occasionally whispering to one another as the hours moved.

Chipper hadn't slept much because he dreaded the morning, the moment when Kyle Lee would find out just how awful his daddy was. Reba hadn't said anything else about the bike, and he appreciated her concern for his feelings. Obviously, she didn't want him to feel any guiltier than he already did. But now the time had come to face his worst sin.

Reba wiped her hands and slipped biscuits into the oven. "You ready?" she asked, her eyes brighter than he thought necessary, given the situation.

He sighed. "He's still got a baseball," he said. "And the clothes and candy."

"He's got plenty," said Reba. "You worked two jobs half the year for all of us. We know you love us."

He nodded and followed her into the kid's bedroom to wake them. Five minutes later, after Kyle Lee had washed up, they all rushed to the Christmas tree to open presents. Andrea Grace came first. And, though she wasn't old enough to know much about any of it, her blue eyes sparkled as they unwrapped her baby doll and lay it in her arms.

Kyle Lee came next. He ripped the paper off the packages, the clothes first, a pair of blue jeans and two flannel shirts. Next came the baseball. He tossed it into the air as he pulled it out, almost hitting the ceiling before it fell back into his hands. His eyes gleaming, he looked back to the tree as if expecting something else to miraculously appear.

His heart breaking, Chipper looked at Reba. As if unable to stand it anymore, she suddenly stood and hurried from the room, her eyes filled with tears. Chipper faced Kyle Lee again.

"Good lookin' baseball," he said, trying to put Kyle Lee's mind off the missing bike. "You be the pitcher with that baseball."

Kyle Lee grinned, but his eyes were still on the tree. Chipper heard the kitchen door open and saw Reba step into the room, her eyes till flooding.

"Hold it right there," she said. "Maybe Santa had to leave one gift outdoors."

Kyle Lee jumped from his seat and Chipper followed him. Reba threw up her hand. "Stay there!" she said. "Right there!"

Pushing the door wider, she reached back and pulled something into the room. Chipper's mouth fell open. Reba had a red bicycle by the handle bars. Kyle Lee ran to it and threw his leg over the seat. Reba walked to Chipper and put her arm around his waist.

"Billy Baldwin," she explained quietly. "He asked me if I wanted it back. I gave him the money Stella found in the bar. We're about three dollars short, but Billy said you could pay him the rest from your first paycheck."

Chipper's mouth fell open even wider. "What paycheck?"

"He wants to hire you. He's almost seventy-five years old and been wanting to retire, but didn't know anybody to take over in the shop. Ty Bo told him he couldn't use you right now. Billy asked if you'd be interested."

"A pawn shop?"

"It's honest work. Besides . . . Billy's made it more of knick-knack shop than anything else over the last few years. Nothing underhanded about any of it."

Chipper's thoughts spun around and around, boggled by the sudden turn of events. He faced Reba again. "So Billy wants me to work for him?"

"Yeah, he'll stay with you for a few months to see how it goes. Then, if it all works, maybe you can take over."

"He got no family?"

"None at all."

Chipper nodded slowly. Why not?

"Look, Dad!"

Chipper turned to Kyle Less as he straddled his bike and pushed it across the floor. "It's just the right size!"

Chipper smiled and stepped to Kyle Lee, lifting him off the bicycle and holding him tight in his arms.

"Just the right size for now!" he said. "But in another couple of years you'll need a new one! You just wait and see." He dropped him back to the floor and turned to Reba.

"You need to open your present," he said, handing her the green-wrapped package from under the tree. "It's not much of a surprise but . . ."

Reba pulled the package from his hand, a pleased smile on her lips. "If you bought what I asked, then you did good." She sat down and slowly unwrapped the package. Inside she found a black leather Bible, it's cover inscribed with gold-colored lettering. Her eyes happy, she leafed through the pages and ran her fingers down the lines. For several seconds, the room fell quiet except for the sounds of Kyle Lee examining his bicycle. Reba flicked to the back of the Bible, the section with an atlas of the biblical world, a short glossary of terms, and almost twenty pages of study notes. Behind the notes, she saw a page full of pictures, each of them a different image of the cross as artists had drawn it over the centuries.

"It's beautiful," she said, running her fingers across

the pictures. "Must have cost you ten dollars at least."

Chipper sat down on the arm of her seat and kissed her on the head. "What it cost don't matter," he said. "Just so you're happy." He stared down at the page. His mouth fell open once more. He studied the images on the paper, one image in particular.

"What's that?" he asked, pointing to the picture.

"It's a cross," said Reba, reading the heading under the image. "Says it's called a 'shepherd's cross.'"

The hair on Chipper's neck stood. His breath came in rapid gulps. The cross had a horizontal piece as usual. But the vertical piece had a crook at the top end that curved to the right and then down like a peppermint stick. Though it wasn't obvious at first glance, it certainly made sense now. The vertical piece was a shepherd's staff, no question about it.

"I've seen that before," he whispered.

"Says here that soldiers wore it on their shields or helmets during the Crusades. Reminded them of God's presence, even in war."

Chipper could hardly speak. "It's . . . it's . . . the necklace," he said.

"What?"

"The shepherd's cross. That's the . . . the wood piece on the necklace . . . the tattoo on the man at the bar . . ."

"The patch on the cape?"

"The same thing."

Chipper took the Bible from Reba, ran his fingers over the cross on the page, read the description underneath it. A shepherd's cross, a reminder of God's presence through life, even in war. He touched his stump to his chest and a hint of his old resentment welled up in his throat.

"God wasn't with me," he whispered. "I lost my arm."

Reba sighed and placed her hand on his. "You did," she said. "But you also came home alive."

He closed his eyes and ran that thought through his head. A very long minute passed. He felt his stomach tighten as he realized he had one of two choices facing him—either hold onto the anger, or decide to leave it in the past. Yes, he could see the loss of his arm as God's failure. Or he could take Reba's option, see his escape from the trap as God's protection. He'd tried the first way for six years. But it had led to nothing but heartache—an addiction to drinking and nearly the loss of his family. And the second way he'd never tried. Maybe it was time. He opened his eyes and faced Reba.

"I did come home," he said, taking her hand and touching it to his cheek. "You're right about that."

"I thank God every day that you did."

"I don't know about God," he said.

"I know. But I can still pray, can't I?"

Chipper touched the picture of the shepherd's cross. Strange things had happened last night, things he couldn't understand and had no way to explain. Maybe Reba's prayers made as much sense as anything.

"Prayer sure can't hurt," he said. "Yeah, pray all you want."

Reba smiled and kissed his hand. Kyle Lee sat on his

bicycle. Andrea Grace slept on the couch.

"I think I'll go look for that cross," said Chipper rising from his seat.

"Hard to find in the snow," said Reba.

Chipper nodded, but grabbed his coat and pulled on his hat anyway. "Back in a few minutes," he said.

"I'll fix some breakfast."

Kissing her on the cheek, he walked out of the house and took a deep breath. The cold air burned into his nose, and he smelled the smoke from his stove. In the yard, the snow crunched under his brogans as he walked toward the stand of trees where he'd thrown the necklace. At the spot where he thought it had landed, he stooped down and ran his fingers over the fresh snow. But he didn't find the necklace. He moved to another spot but still had no luck. Standing, he rubbed a foot across the snow, digging under the surface. But no necklace appeared.

Pausing, he took off his cap and stared into it as if expecting to see the answers to all the riddles of the universe inside. He thought of Mose, Gabe and Mikey. Strangers in the night, mysterious messengers tied together by something so unusual that he couldn't believe it had actually happened. Chipper grunted and jammed his head back into his hat. Maybe it hadn't. Maybe he drank more than he realized, maybe a trio of hallucinations had overwhelmed him, a mix-up of his subconscious trying to carry him a message. He studied the snow again but still saw nothing. He heard a door open, then heard Reba calling him from the porch.

"Eggs about ready!" she called. "Come on in."

Chipper smiled. Overhead the sun broke through the clouds. He stared down at the snow once more. Maybe he'd never find the necklace, he figured—never have any tangible evidence of the events of last night. But maybe that didn't matter. Maybe what mattered was that he had heard what the night had told him. He had to change, had to leave the war behind, escape its grip as he had escaped the trap that had taken his arm.

He bent down and picked up a handful of snow. He loved it like this—so clean and unmarked. He tossed it back to the ground, brushing off his hands. He could start over, he decided, like the fresh snow—become a new man; not naive like a ten-year-old boy, but changed just the same. He had a wife and children who loved him and needed him. And maybe God did watch over him, he'd have to consider that carefully.

He looked at his stump for a moment. For the first time ever, he realized what could have happened. He could have lost his life in the jungle, could be there still, a man lost to wife and family forever, a casualty of the worst evil that human beings can do.

He stared off into the woods. Whether God had brought him home or not he didn't know. But he was home. Maybe a piece of arm wasn't too high a price to pay. He heard the door open and saw Kyle Lee and Thumper running his way, Reba with Andrea Grace in her arms following them. Kyle Lee picked up a handful of snow, rubbed it into a snowball and threw it at him.

His laugh ringing out into the empty trees, Chipper

grabbed some snow and headed toward his son, his heart so light it seemed to have turned to air. Heaving the snowball, he ran to Kyle Lee and whirled him up and around and around. A snowball hit him in the back, and he twisted to see Reba headed his way, Andrea Grace on her hip. "You'll pay for that," he shouted at her, grabbing for more snow. Reba's laughter joined his and the sound of it mixed together and skipped across the hills of Buckview. And a deer almost half a mile away lifted its head to listen.

EPILOGUE

Thirty two years later

Sometimes when you've told a tale that cuts you deep, you wonder if you should have completed it. Why not just leave it all in the dark, hidden in the basement places that never see the sun, to never breathe the air of spoken truth? I expect that's what most folks do, and I can't rightly blame 'em. Revealing hurtful tales, even when they eventually turned out for the better, wrenches us at the core; and nobody likes the way that feels while it's happening. But in spite of that, I've told you the story of my daddy Chipper Gaines. I've said it all, everything that happened, no matter how painful it is to look it in the eye again.

I have my reasons for this, of course. Partly to make sure I've finished up my own dealings with it. I'm forty-two now, and one year removed from my daddy's death. So I figure it's time for me to tidy up the remaining pieces of my own childhood hurts, my own skins and scrapes. People keep telling me that talking things out helps do that. So, even though my daddy never took another drink after the Christmas he gave me that red bicycle, I needed to speak it out one more time to make sure I'm all done with it.

Not only that, but it's come to me lately that my tale might make a difference for someone else, some other child with a family pulling apart at the seams because of some demon evil grabbing at a parent, some mean-spirited serpent the parent can't seem to subdue. I don't know if that's true or not, but it does seem that when we know that somebody else has stared down a monster—it helps when our turn comes to do the same. Least ways, that's my hope.

Some of what I told you probably dug in at your squeamishness just a touch, especially when I talked about the war. What goes on between fighting men on bloody battlefields makes even the strongest of heart all shuddery and faint. But I couldn't tell the tale without that part. The only way to understand my daddy's weakness for the bottle was to know what happened the day he lost his arm. Thankfully, though, the losing of the arm wasn't all the story.

I can't think of much else to say before you close the page. Only that I didn't know all of this back when it first happened. Mama and Daddy told me the story later, after I had matured to the point of understanding. All I knew at the time was that everything changed after that Christmas, everything about Mama and Daddy, everything about me.

We still don't know the identity of the three who spoke that difference into being. Like wisps of wood smoke that appear over a chimney for an instant and then vanish, the change-makers visited my daddy's life for just that one night, a night all dark and eerie, not like a night you usually think of when Christmas enters your mind. That night was as different when it came as we were after the next day's sunshine pushed it away. But sometimes that's what we need for anything new to happen—a night when nothing seems right at first.

Sometimes I still look for Mose, Gabe, and Mikey. I wonder if they might one day show their faces again. But that's an altogether unrelated matter . . . not for the telling today.

One last thing—the preacher baptized Daddy and me exactly five years after I got my bicycle. Both of us took the dip on the same day in May in a creek so cold it made the preacher's teeth chatter. Mama sang "Amazing Grace," and that afternoon Daddy told me the story of the shepherd's cross. At first I didn't know whether or not to believe what he said. I mean, after all, he did suck down a good bit of liquor that evening. Easy enough to pass off what he said as the visions of a man heavy under the influence. But one thing I did know was true—whether it happened like my daddy said or not, something caused an alteration in his heart that night. That had to be something mighty powerful.

I saw Daddy out in the yard on his next to last day of living. He had a cane in his hand, and his eyes were searching the ground beside the house he built on the same ground as the one in which I grew up. I knew what he was looking for—the same thing he'd tried to find off and on ever since he threw it out that Christmas Eve—the shepherd's cross. He never found it, of course. Like the messengers who brought it . . . it had just simply disappeared.

I own the house now. Andrea Grace lives a half mile down the road, and my baby brother Bailey, Jr., about the same distance past her. From time to time we all talk about it, that Christmas of 1951, six years after my daddy came home from the war. That year I got the best gift a boy could ever imagine. And I'm not talking about my bicycle . . .